Herbs

Other Publications:

Herbs

by
JAMES UNDERWOOD CROCKETT,
OGDEN TANNER
and
the Editors of TIME-LIFE BOOKS

Watercolor Illustrations by
Richard Crist

TIME-LIFE BOOKS, ALEXANDRIA, VIRGINIA

CO-AUTHOR: The late James Underwood Crockett was an eminent horticulturist, writer on gardening and, on television, a teacher of plant care. A graduate of the University of Massachusetts' Stockbridge School of Agriculture, he received an Honorary Doctor of Science degree from the University of Massachusetts at Amherst and was cited by the American Association of Nurserymen and the American Horticultural Society. He worked with plants in California, New York, Texas and New England. He wrote books on greenhouse, indoor and window-sill gardening, a monthly column for *Horticulture* magazine and a monthly bulletin, "Flowery Talks," for florists. His weekly television program, *Crockett's Victory Garden,* was broadcast throughout the United States.

CO-AUTHOR: Ogden Tanner, a freelance writer and former editor of THE TIME-LIFE ENCYCLOPEDIA OF GARDENING, also wrote *New England Wilds* and *Urban Wilds* for THE AMERICAN WILDERNESS series and volumes on history, nature, science and photography. An architectural graduate of Princeton University, he has been associate editor of *House & Home* and assistant managing editor of *Architectural Forum*. He has written articles on landscape architecture and is an amateur botanist and weekend gardener.

ILLUSTRATOR: Richard Crist provided the watercolor paintings for this book and for *Vegetables and Fruits* for THE TIME-LIFE ENCYCLOPEDIA OF GARDENING. He studied at Carnegie Institute of Technology and The Art Institute of Chicago. An amateur botanist, Mr. Crist is author of several children's books.

GENERAL CONSULTANTS: Louise and Cyrus Hyde, Well-Sweep Herb Farm, Port Murray, New Jersey; George A. Kalmbacher, Plant Taxonomist, Brooklyn Botanic Garden, Brooklyn, New York; Joy Logee Martin, Logee's Greenhouses, Danielson, Connecticut; Adelma Grenier Simmons, Caprilands Herb Farm, North Coventry, Connecticut.

THE COVER: Interlacing bands of germander, winter savory, green and gray lavender cotton herbs shape the traditional knot garden at the Brooklyn Botanic Garden. The garden is patterned on one at Britain's royal residence at Hampton Court that probably dates from the reign of Elizabeth I. Between the bands are marble chips, coal and clay shards. The polka dots are dwarf boxwood.

CONTENTS

Plants of many virtues 1

If you are like most people, you probably have a few containers marked *Basil, Oregano* or *Rosemary* on a kitchen shelf, handy to add sparkle to a tomato sauce or a roast. You may even keep a pot of chives growing fresh on a sunny window sill to snip into cottage cheese or Sunday morning scrambled eggs, or a patch of mint outdoors for juleps or iced tea. That, until recently, was the extent of general interest in herbs. But no longer. Today the experience of one young gardener is more typical.

She saw a classified ad under "Herbs" in a garden magazine and decided to send for a few new plants. Over the next year or two she added to her plot and before long she was growing 30 different culinary herbs near her kitchen door. Furthermore, she learned how to use each of them—at their fresh and flavorful best—to lend a personal touch to her salads, soups and stews, and in the process she created a few unique recipes.

Soon she found that herbs provided more than culinary pleasures. In a sunny spot in her yard, she planted her own miniature version of an Elizabethan knot garden, an ingenious bit of horticultural geometry in which the rich greens and silvery grays of germanders and artemisias intertwined around a sundial framed by fragrant thymes and a low lavender hedge. Indoors, she made scented mixtures of dried lavender and other herbs, and created eye-pleasing arrangements of fresh and dried herbs.

Not everyone, of course, gets quite so engrossed in herbs as this gardener. But in recent years a growing number of amateurs have taken up herb growing as a hobby, including many who previously had little experience with plants of any kind.

No one has inventoried the number of home herb gardens that have been planted, but one recent five-year period saw a doubling of the number of requests for information that reached harried officials of the Herb Society of America, a doubling in the quantity

Two bearded scholars and an apprentice harvest herbs in a woodcut illustrating a 13th Century German manuscript on medicinal plants. The tree is probably the artist's imaginative rendering of a palm.

of dried herbs sold in retail food stores, and a doubling in the sale of herb plants by specialized nurseries across the country. At the National Cathedral in Washington, D.C., which has its own herb garden, greenhouse and herb shop, sales quadrupled in that time.

Statistics of the American Spice Trade Association encompass not only the tropical aromatics usually thought of as spices, such as cinnamon and nutmeg, but many herb flavorings as well. Between 1970 and 1975, total consumption of such spices in the United States increased 33 per cent over the preceding five years, to almost 30 ounces per person each year. Oregano and sesame seed accounted for a good portion of this gain (the increase in oregano consumption paralleled the growth in the popularity of pizza). About one fourth of the spices consumed in the United States were grown here rather than in the tropics, including great quantities of basil, parsley, sage, mustard seed, dill, fennel and sesame.

BEHIND THE BOOM The modern interest in herbs undoubtedly arises partly from a new consciousness of nature and a desire to return to a more natural way of life. Part, too, stems from dissatisfaction with the blandness of some modern foods and a desire to stretch ordinary budgets and ingredients into gourmet meals at home. But many people grow herbs simply because it is fun. Of all plants, none offers such great rewards for so little work. Many are decorative, indoors and out, and they are easy to grow and resistant to diseases and pests. Some are highly fragrant, bursting with sweet oils.

Herbs keep on providing their pleasures right through the year. Many kinds can spend the winter indoors growing on a sunny window sill, while the leaves or seeds of others can be dried or frozen for a year-round supply that retains much of its original garden-fresh taste. Beyond the kitchen uses, a scented geranium or a potpourri of rose petals brings to a living room reminders of summer that no canned room freshener can match; a sachet of dried lavender or rosemary leaves lends a clean fragrance to a linen drawer and keeps moths from woolens; wreaths and other dried arrangements lend a festive air to a holiday table, as does a punch bowl flavored with borage, sweet woodruff or lemon balm.

That so many different and delightful purposes can be served by herbs is not surprising. More than a thousand herbs are still being cultivated; the Indiana Botanic Gardens in Hammond sells that many, most of them imported from Europe and South America. In the encyclopedia section of this book *(page 91),* 126 herbs suitable for the United States are illustrated and described.

To the ancients, any plant that was not a shrub or a tree was considered an herb—and a suitable candidate for experimentation to see what use might be made of it. To botanists, any plant that dies down to the ground after its growing season, and, if it is a perennial, sprouts again the following spring, is technically an herb. But to most people, an herb is a plant, generally small and easy to cultivate, that offers a special usefulness. It may be grown primarily for its fragrance, or for its value in cooking or for its historical associations, particularly with medicine—many are practical remedies and many more were once thought to be.

The broad range of species that, by one definition or another, could be counted as herbs poses a puzzle for the beginning gardener. Where do you start? One Philadelphia matron, inspired by a lecture on herbs to plant her own herb garden, sought advice from the gardener-handyman who kept her rose beds in order and her boxwood trimmed. The man put down his spading fork, rubbed his chin thoughtfully, then said, "Plant a little mint, missus. Then step out of the way so you don't get hurt."

The advice was not as impertinent as it might sound. Of all herbs, the common mint is not only among the most popular—a favorite flavoring for drinks and sauces—but among the most prolific, easy to grow even for people without green thumbs. Indeed, unless it is contained within a barricade, it will spread by underground runners and may take over half the yard, cheerfully coming up year after year whether you want it to or not.

To the handyman's terse nominee for instant success might be added a few other reliables among the perennial culinary herbs: chives, tarragon, sage, oregano and thyme, for example. All can be started from seeds (except true French tarragon, which, unlike the inferior-tasting Russian tarragon, rarely produces viable seeds and is usually grown from stem cuttings taken from existing plants). To an impatient gardener-gourmet, however, these perennial herbs and many others, including mint, seem to take forever to grow large enough to harvest when grown from seed. It is easier as well as quicker to buy nursery-grown perennial plants that can be enjoyed the first year.

THE FAST-GROWING ANNUALS

To round out a basic herb garden, you will want to include some of the annual and biennial herbs as well, perhaps parsley, basil, summer savory, dill and sweet marjoram. (The latter is a perennial that will not survive the winter in cold climates and thus is grown as an annual in northern zones.) These herbs too can usually be bought as young plants, but it is not difficult—and considerably cheaper—to start them from seeds. Unlike many perennials, the annuals will

HERB OR 'ERB?

How do you pronounce "herb?" Though some people contend that "erb," with the H dropped, is preferable, "herb" with a hard H is also correct. "Erb" is the older pronunciation, and is more common on the North American side of the Atlantic, while "herb" has gained wider usage in England, where ladies and gentlemen would just as soon not be suspected of having a cockney accent.

grow fast enough in one season to provide all the flavoring ingredients you will need.

But an herb garden ought not to be restricted to old favorites used to enhance other foodstuffs. Many gardeners include lesser known but equally rewarding edible herbs that in certain dishes may become principal ingredients, not just flavoring.

For those who enjoy salads, there is nothing quite so satisfying as a garden of the herbs that turn everyday salads into extraordinary treats. Among the fresh young leaves that can be used for greens are burnet, borage, lovage, chervil, mustard, orach, sorrel and sweet cicely. Even plants like chicory and dandelion, often thought of as weeds, are tasty greens—dandelions have been a

PLANNING AND PLANTING A CLASSIC KNOT GARDEN

The knot garden design at right is an adaptation of a traditional 16th Century plan. Only three varieties of herbs are needed to create what appears to be a complex pattern of interwoven ribbons, characteristic of this kind of ornamental garden. An easy way to lay out this geometric design is illustrated step-by-step opposite.

When you choose herbs for a knot garden, select compact, low-growing perennials that will tolerate frequent pruning. Among such plants are dwarf lavender, germander, the low-growing artemisias, lemon thyme, hyssop, dwarf sage and santolina. Place the selected plants very close together, at 3- or 4-inch intervals, so the immediate effect will be one of a continuous ribbon. Then prune them all to a uniform height except where the rows intersect. There the ribbon that is meant to look as if it is on top should be shaped with the pruning shears to give the illusion that it sweeps up and over the lower ribbon.

An established knot garden needs to be manicured on a regular schedule through the growing season in order to keep the ribbon design sharp and clear at all times.

Contrasting colors and textures of the foliage emphasize the over-and-underlapping motif of this design. Before you begin planting a knot garden, make a diagram like this, coloring and labeling each ribbon.

favorite since colonial days, and the leaves look and taste better if you buy quality seeds and plant them in their own garden bed with enriched soil. Garden cress or nasturtiums—both the leaves and flowers of the latter—add a peppery tang and an attractive garnish; violet leaves and flowers lend a pleasant perfumed taste; rue satisfies those who like a bitter bite, but be warned that a little goes a long way. Cardoon and fennel have tasty stalks, and the various onions like garlic, chives, shallots, leeks and Egyptian onions add distinctive piquancies of their own.

Many an herb enthusiast devotes part of his herb garden, or a small separate garden, to herbs especially noted for their scents. Walking among such plants on a summer evening can be a heady

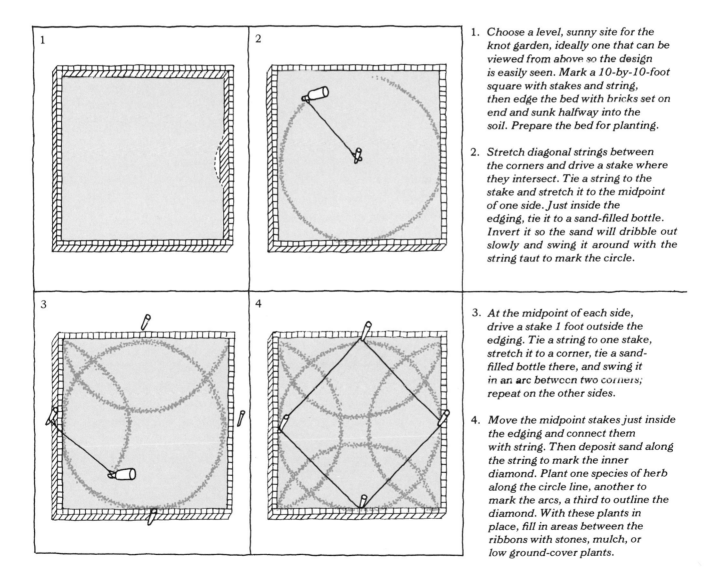

1. Choose a level, sunny site for the knot garden, ideally one that can be viewed from above so the design is easily seen. Mark a 10-by-10-foot square with stakes and string, then edge the bed with bricks set on end and sunk halfway into the soil. Prepare the bed for planting.

2. Stretch diagonal strings between the corners and drive a stake where they intersect. Tie a string to the stake and stretch it to the midpoint of one side. Just inside the edging, tie it to a sand-filled bottle. Invert it so the sand will dribble out slowly and swing it around with the string taut to mark the circle.

3. At the midpoint of each side, drive a stake 1 foot outside the edging. Tie a string to one stake, stretch it to a corner, tie a sand-filled bottle there, and swing it in an arc between two corners; repeat on the other sides.

4. Move the midpoint stakes just inside the edging and connect them with string. Then deposit sand along the string to mark the inner diamond. Plant one species of herb along the circle line, another to mark the arcs, a third to outline the diamond. With these plants in place, fill in areas between the ribbons with stones, mulch, or low ground-cover plants.

experience, particularly when you brush against the leaves and release the full aroma of their oils. Some of these oils are useful in flavoring, but the fragrance of almost any of them can be captured for later enjoyment by drying the leaves and flower petals for potpourris, scented pillows and sachets. Among the mainstays of a fragrance garden are old-fashioned, sweet-smelling bush roses, useful as accents or in hedges; lavender, for lower hedges, borders or beds; some of the pungent mints, especially the delicate apple mint; and the most fragrant sages and thymes. There are also lemon verbena and rosemary, which smell as good as they taste, and many kinds of scented geraniums with fragrances suggesting those of roses, lemons and spices. However, lemon verbena, rosemary and scented geranium will live through the winter only in warmer climates; in colder areas they must be moved indoors in the fall.

BEAUTY WITH PRACTICALITY   Still other herbs are prized not so much for their flavors or fragrances as for their decorative appearance. At one time or another many had household or medicinal uses, but today they are grown mainly for their colors and textures. Notable among these plants are those associated with the so-called gray or silver garden, a specialty since Elizabethan times. Because the leaves have arresting silvery colors—some finely fernlike or softly hairy and appearing nearly white in bright sunlight—they provide stunning garden accents in themselves and serve as foils for herbs with darker foliage or bright blooms. The effect of silver plantings can be especially lovely, almost eerie, at night, when the leaves reflect the faintest sky glow; for this reason they are sometimes called moonlight gardens. Among the herbs most used are the various artemisias—southernwood, wormwood, the tall feathery Silver King and the low-clustered Silver Mound—as well as lavender, lavender cotton, dittany, lamb's ears, woolly mint and silver thyme.

For contrast with the silver species, dark green plants like low-growing germander are often used in borders. These darker herbs also often make up one strand of a knot design, interwoven with a light-colored row of dwarf santolinas or other light-gray plants that can easily be kept neatly clipped. Striking contrasts can also be provided by yellow-orange calendulas, old favorites in herb gardens, or the purple foliage of Dark Opal basil or red orach. Some connoisseurs, however, prefer to keep the whole garden a subtle palette of gray and silver accented by a few shades of green.

Even more specialized gardens are possible with herbs. One type is the bee garden, filled with such plants as bee balm, lemon balm, thyme and borage, which are particularly attractive to honeybees (more than one herb gardener has taken up beekeeping as a hobby for the tasty honey thus produced). Some herbalists raise plants like woad, bedstraw, tansy, alkanet and rue to make natural vegetable dyes. Others set aside a corner for the materials of herbal teas—chamomile, catnip, sage, lemon verbena and several of the mints. Still others, delving into history, have modeled herb beds after those of medieval monasteries or colonial dooryards; a few specialists even try to grow all the herbs mentioned in the Bible or in Shakespeare's plays—and quote appropriate passages as proof.

It is such historical associations, perhaps, that give herbs their ultimate appeal. Most of them are old-fashioned plants, not showy crossbreeds of the modern era, and they go back a lot further than Aunt Minnie's lavender sachets or Aunt Mabel's rose-water bath. Herbs are, in fact, the oldest cultivated garden species in the world. As such, they offer the interested amateur entertaining glimpses of the way people lived in days gone by—not only hundreds but thousands of years ago. Herbs are living windows on the past.

REFLECTIONS OF DAYS PAST

    In the old days all manner of plants were used not only for their flavors and scents but for almost everything else under the sun—witches' potions, aphrodisiacs, invigorating teas, remedies for upset stomachs and falling hair, healing salves for wounds, agents to fend off plague and pestilence, deodorizers to disguise indoor smells. Rudyard Kipling once observed: "Anything green that grew out of the mold/Was an excellent herb to our fathers of old." (And he added wryly: "Half of their remedies cured you dead.")

    Until the advent of modern synthetic drugs, scarcely more than a century ago, most medical therapy was based on plants. Ancient records indicate that 5,000 years ago the Sumerians had medicinal uses for caraway and thyme, and a Chinese manuscript of 2700 B.C. listed 365 plants and their health-giving qualities (including a shrub called mahuang, or ephedra, from which chemists derive the modern nasal decongestant ephedrine). A thousand years before Christ, Egyptian kings fed their slaves and laborers quantities of garlic in the belief that it would make them strong enough to build the pyramids. The Bible suggests that anise and cumin seeds, among others, were of such medicinal value that they were sometimes used to pay debts.

In later centuries the Greeks and Romans expanded and codified the uses of herbs. One of their favorites was an evergreen they called laurel, which grows to tree size on the sunny Mediterranean shores—the same *Laurus nobilis* used today under the name of

FROM GARLAND TO STEW

The gray-green foliage of some 70 different
herbs shimmers whitely in the sun and appears
silvery by moonlight in herbalist Adelma
Simmons' "gray garden." Designed as a soothing
contrast to the intense colors of nearby flower
beds, her planting includes velvety lamb's ears
surrounded by feathery santolina around a
statue of Pan, blue-flowered lavender and a
group of sages in the front corner, and along
the back at the right, a semicircle of artemisias
backed by blue-green junipers.

sweet bay to flavor stuffings and stews (not the familiar American mountain laurel, whose leaves are toxic). Legend had it that the gods turned the nymph Daphne into a laurel tree to save her from the clutches of Apollo; laurel was regarded as divine, and leafy twigs of it were woven into garlands to crown victorious warriors and athletes as well as eloquent statesmen and poets. At festivals, youths and maidens wore ceremonial garlands of other herbs, including parsley, dill and fennel—the latter celebrating the triumphant Battle of Marathon. (Marathon means fennel in Greek; on a field of fennel, the Greeks defeated a Persian army in 490 B.C.)

The Romans, who perpetuated and elaborated many Greek traditions, also used fennel for ceremonial garlands, and valued its fresh, licorice flavor when it was cooked or chopped into salads. The Romans scattered powdered herbs about their houses and often burned them as incense—the word perfume comes from the Latin *per fumum,* literally "by smoke." They crushed the flowers of one fragrant species into their bath water so frequently that it became known as lavender, after the Latin *lavare,* to bathe.

The Greeks and Romans also started the custom, continued throughout Europe and elsewhere until modern times, of using aromatic plants like lavender, mint and thyme as strewing herbs, meant to be spread on floors so their fragrance would cover household odors. One of the most treasured of the aromatics—in fact, the greatest status symbol among herbs—was saffron, a golden, sweet-scented powder from the flower stigmas of the saffron crocus. Since it takes some 65,000 hand-picked blossoms to make a pound of saffron, its use became the epitome of conspicuous consumption, and the wealthy employed it to flavor their food, perfume their banquet halls and dye their robes. The Emperor Nero, with typical extravagance, ordered saffron water sprinkled along the road before him when he made his triumphal entries into Rome.

PLANTS THAT SOOTHE

But herbs were prized most of all for their medicinal virtues, real or imagined. The first physicians were avid herbalists; Hippocrates, known as the father of medicine, described some 400 medicinal herbs used in his day, including basil, horehound, rue and sage. The oldest major treatise on the uses of healing plants, called *De Materia Medica,* was compiled in the First Century A.D. by Dioscorides, a Greek physician serving with Roman armies. It remained an authoritative work for the next 1500 years. In Dioscorides' view, herbs were remarkably versatile in their medical applications. For example, mountain rue, which makes some people violently ill, could, in his opinion, cure poisoning, snakebite, chest pain, hard breathing, coughing, lung inflammation, worms, stones, poor vision, headache, nosebleed, and pain in the hips, joints and ears. Cress was prescribed to break up carbuncles, cure falling hair, stimulate passion and drive away serpents. Garlic, Dioscorides reported, worked wonders in treating boils, coughs, lice, ulcers, toothache and dog bites. The lily removed wrinkles, ivy turned the hair black, and cinquefoil soothed or cured toothache, dysentery, liver and lung diseases, poisons, wounds, fear and enchantment.

Of all the herbs valued by the ancients, rosemary was perhaps the most versatile and beloved. This aromatic shrub with soft, flat green needles grew on the spray-swept headlands of the Mediterranean—and was christened *ros marinus,* "dew of the sea." It was used in fragrant hedges and borders in the walled gardens of Egypt, Algeria and Spain; the Greeks wore it in festive garlands, burned it at sacrifices and strewed it on floors. Like many other herbs still in use today, it traveled north across Europe and Britain with the Roman legions, becoming a salve for wounds, a love potion, an ingredient in perfumes and embalming fluids, a savory for meats, and one of 130-odd herbs thought to flavor the Carthusian monks' secret formula for chartreuse liqueur. In the 13th Century, Queen Elizabeth of Hungary made famous a concoction called Hungary Water—rosemary, lavender and myrtle steeped in brandy; later, rosemary became a constituent of eau de cologne.

> **THE DEW OF THE SEA**

Throughout history rosemary appears and reappears as the major herb of sentiment, an evergreen symbol believed to strengthen the bonds of love. Shakespeare's Ophelia declared to Laertes: "There's rosemary, that's for remembrance; pray, love, remember," and the body of the fair Juliet was borne to church covered with sprigs of the herb. In many parts of the world today rosemary still decorates the hearth at Christmas, is slipped into bridal bouquets, and at funerals is placed lovingly in the hands of the dead.

During the Dark Ages in Europe, the lore of rosemary and many other herbs was kept alive in monasteries, where monks diligently copied recipes from ancient herbals and tended gardens of medicinal plants, which they used in their hospitals to treat the sick. Outside monastery walls itinerant herbalists wandered through the villages selling herbs, along with secret formulas and incantations to make them work. Around 800 A.D. the French king, Charlemagne, compiled an official list of herbs to be planted by his subjects for their well-being, and ordered the plants grown in the royal gardens as well. To him is attributed a classic definition of an herb: "The friend of the physician and the pride of cooks."

A Renaissance garden

In 1545 Francesco Bonafede, professor of botany in the medical school of northern Italy's University of Padua, persuaded the local government to establish a Garden of Simples, or herb garden, so his students could practice on the plants of which he preached. Spread over three acres leased from a nearby monastery, the garden's modest collection of plants grew over the years.

The garden introduced to Europe such exotica as the potato, the sunflower and the sesame. One of its possessions, a European fan palm, particularly fascinated the poet Goethe, who visited in 1786; he wrote a dissertation on the palm, noting that its leaves were different in form, bottom and top. Goethe's palm still stands, labeled as such. And on marble tablets at the garden's entrance can be seen Professor Bonafede's rules for the garden's use: visitors are cautioned not to break stems or branches, pick flowers or collect seeds—on pain of being fined, imprisoned or banished.

A 16th Century plan of the Spaldo Terzo, or Third Bed, below, identifies the garden's plantings in terms that no longer correspond to modern plant names (and are, moreover, almost illegible).

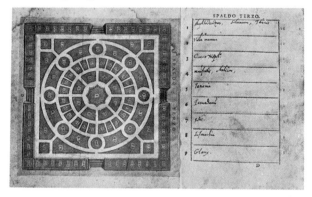

In an 1854 overview of the garden, the main gate is at the top, flanked by a semicircular row of greenhouses that no longer exist. During this period, the garden contained 16,000 kinds of plants, more than it holds today.

In the modern garden, a circular greenhouse protects Goethe's palm, now grown to great size. The semicircular beds directly in front of it hold the garden's only remaining herbs, originally its raison d'être.

Terraced plots of herbs now growing in the garden include spearlike mullein, lower right, and, beside it, blue-flowered hyssop. To the left of the hyssop is white-flowered henbane and, at the upper left, curly-leaved horseradish.

19

With the invention of printing in the 15th Century, herbs and herbalists entered their golden age. Over the next two centuries hundreds of different herbals were published, books propounding ancient wisdom spiced with the latest discoveries, theories and opinions. The best known early work in English was *The Grete Herball* of 1526, a translation of a French book that promised a "parfyt knowledge and understanding of all manner of herbes and there gracyous vertues." Even more celebrated were William Turner's *Herball,* published in three installments between 1551 and 1562, and *The Herball or Generall Historie of Plantes,* completed in 1597 by John Gerard, an English barber-surgeon with a passion for gardening and an eye for fame. (Hired to translate a Belgian work, he rearranged it and, with the help of 1,800 woodcuts borrowed from a German botanical treatise, published it as his own.) In 1640 John Parkinson, another gardener-physician who was official herbalist to King Charles I, published his *Theatrum Botanicum,* a stupendous work that examined the characteristics and uses of no fewer than 3,800 species.

AN ELIZABETHAN HERBAL The most popular herbal of all, however, was a slimmer volume by a 33-year-old apothecary and astrologer named Nicholas Culpeper, who in 1649 outraged England's learned College of Physicians by translating their precious pharmacopeia—an exclusive tome consulted only by doctors who could read Latin—into plain English, with critical comments of his own, for common folk to share. The brash Culpeper followed in 1653 with his chef-d'oeuvre, *The English Physician,* which bore the clarion, non-stop title: *An Astrological Discourse of the Vulgar Herbs of this Nation being a Compleat Method of Physick whereby a man may preserve his Body in health; or cure himself being sick, for three pence charge, with such things one-ly as grow in England, they being most fit for English Bodies.* A spirited blend of traditional medicine, folklore, astrology and magic, it listed 369 plants along with detailed advice on where to find each, how to recognize it, which celestial body it was governed by and the uses it might have.

Culpeper was not only brash; he had a ready wit with which to present an astonishing amount of information—and misinformation. About a concoction that incorporated mustard seed, he wrote: "Let old men and women make much of this Medicine, and they will either give me thanks or manifest ingratitude." At another point he noted: "Sage is of excellent use to help the Memory, warming and quickening the senses; and the Conserve made of the Flowers is used to the same purpose."

Among the more curious gospels preached by Culpeper and others in their herbals was the Doctrine of Signatures, which held that the proper medicinal use of a plant could be divined from its appearance. Thus the signature attributed to a species known as lungwort—vaguely lung-shaped leaves covered with whitish spots—supposedly indicated that it could be used for treatment of diseased, i.e., spotted, lungs. It was steeped in infusions and quaffed by uncounted numbers of Britons for the treatment of chest colds and whooping cough. In the same way wild pansies were regarded as a potent base for a heart tonic because they have heart-shaped leaves; hollow-stalked plants like garlic were believed salutary for ailments of the windpipe; the flowers of eyebright, thought to resemble bloodshot eyes, were used to make eye lotions for preventing blindness and curing cataracts.

Even odder, though more innocent, meanings were attached to herbs in the Language of Flowers, an elaborate code of symbols that started in the Middle Ages and reached its peak in romantic Victorian days. In this courtly and circumspect method of communication, a lady and her suitor—presumably both armed with the same list of plants and their assigned meanings, not to mention an ability to recognize different species on sight—could conduct discreet conversations by exchanging appropriate flowers or sprigs.

An eager swain, for example, might open the dialogue by sending his love a sprig of myrtle (symbol, Fragrance; code words, "Be my love"). Or he might pick vervain (Enchantment: "You have bewitched me") or fraxinella (Ardor: "My heart is afire"). If the lady was unimpressed, she might send back lavender (Sad Refusal: "I like you, but only as a friend"); mint (Homeliness: "Find a spouse of your own age and background"); aconite (Dislike: "Your attentions are unwelcome"); or—the unkindest cut of all—the lowly dandelion (Absurdity: "I find your presumption laughable"). If the suitor was undismayed by such chilly responses, he might attempt to rescue the romance with burdock (Persistence: "I shall not be discouraged"). The lady, in turn, could reply with borage (Brusqueness: "Your attentions only embarrass me"); chamomile (Fortitude: "I admire your courage; do not despair"); goldenrod (Indecision: "Allow me time to decide"); or marjoram (Maidenly Innocence: "Your passion sends blushes to my cheeks"). If all went well, a suitor both ardent and tenacious might one day be so fortunate as to experience the spine-tingling moment when the postman arrived with a little envelope containing angelica (Inspiration: "Your love is my guiding star").

Such fripperies as the Language of Flowers were far from the

OLD-TIME AIR FRESHENERS

It was common practice in England as late as the 19th Century to strew aromatic herbs such as marjoram, mint or sweet flag on the floors of modest dwellings and great public buildings alike, in the belief that the scent prevented the spread of disease. During plagues, the sale of such strewing herbs quickened. But the importance attached to them is perhaps best indicated by the prominence given, for centuries, to the role of the herb strewer in the coronations of English kings and queens. Ladies of the court competed fiercely for the honor of leading the royal procession to Westminster Abbey, scattering herbs from a satin-lined gilt basket—a ritual that was intended to purify the air surrounding the monarch. Though the custom died out at the end of the 19th Century, Queen Elizabeth II paid lip service to it by accepting a nosegay of aromatic herbs at her 1953 coronation.

In Elizabethan England many herbs were thought efficacious in warding off disease. Ladies and gentlemen who were forced to frequent streets and public halls of London—hardly models of cleanliness in those days—carried nosegays of lavender, wormwood and other scented leaves, which they sniffed periodically to fend off unpleasant odors and, they hoped, the plagues and poxes that might lurk behind them. Eminent judges in robes and powdered wigs, obliged to share their courtrooms with unsavory criminals on trial, kept similar herbal bouquets handy. And everywhere in those days before preservatives and refrigeration, herbs and spices were doused on food— often in quantities and combinations that would make a modern gourmet gag—to disguise the flavor of tainted if not downright rotten meat.

NOSTRUMS FOR ONE AND ALL

concerns of the first English colonists who came to the shores of America. With them came seeds, roots and cuttings of their favorite household herbs, to be planted in dooryard gardens. Sometimes these were combined with native herbal medicines adopted from the Indians' stock. Every Puritan housewife knew, in John Parkinson's phrase, "what Herbes and Fruits were fit, eyther for meate or medicine, for Use or Delight." She could grow almost every plant she needed: flavorings, garnishes and "sallets" for the table; nosegays and strewing herbs for freshening chambers; repellents for ants, moths, mice and snakes; dyes to color woolens and teasel for teasing up their naps; soothing hot teas of chamomile, sage or wintergreen; plasters, salves and lotions for treating cuts, relieving coughs or toothaches, or easing the pains of childbirth; and, inevitably, herbs for laying out the dead.

Among the colonial New England housewife's "simples"—old reliables used by themselves—were balm for bee stings, elecampane for throat and lung ailments, tansy for treating worms. For more complex "unknown guests," as ailments were called, a package remedy was often deemed appropriate, on the theory that a combination of herbs could purge "both upwards and downwards" by inducing sneezing, sweating, vomiting and laxative action— sometimes all at once. If the patient recovered, the "imbalance" had been eliminated. If he did not, it was believed, God had obviously called him. Some early American recipes were formidable: "Take for a cough or stitch upon a cold, Wormwood, Sage, Marygolds, and Crabs-claws boiled in posset-drink [hot milk curdled by ale or wine and spiced] and drunk off very warm." Or, "For wind Collick, take Summer Savory, Angelica, Sweet Tansy and Elecampane; for back pains, make a syrup of Borage or Comphrey and add Brandy and Gunpowder to taste."

As immigrants arrived from other countries, they brought their own folk medicines. Old Pennsylvania Dutch treatments for asthma, for example, included sleeping on the dried flowers of pearly everlasting, chewing calamus root; smoking the leaves of mullein, drinking teas made of horehound, hyssop, sage, and yarrow, and sipping a potion made by steeping "four quarts of huckleberries for four days in two gallons of good gin." By the 19th Century, commercial herb farms, started modestly by religious communities of Shakers, had begun to supply home remedies that city dwellers could no longer conveniently grow. Before long, hundreds of patent medicines, root tonics and snake oils, most of them using herbs, were advertised in newspapers and sold from door to door.

It is only in this century that herbs have been largely replaced by synthetic drugs in the manufacture of medicines. In fact, many herbal remedies remain in the prescription books of the Caswell-Massey apothecary, founded in 1752 in Newport, Rhode Island, and now in New York City. Milton Taylor, manager of the apothecary since 1936, once displayed an old prescription book from the 1880s. An elderly passerby asked him to duplicate a certain cough medicine visible in the open book.

"There were 27 herbs in that prescription—things like calendula, verbascum, myrrh and benzoin," said Taylor. "I boiled up the decoction myself and kept wondering why he wanted that particular formula." His puzzlement was resolved when the customer, with a gleam of nostalgia in his eye, told him the prescription bore his name and had been written for him some 70 years previously, when he was five years old. Taylor noted that the original prescription carried the notation "p.p.," indicating the patient was from a poor family and the price should be kept down; the new order for the old remedy was delivered to a luxurious suite in the Waldorf Towers on Park Avenue.

THE BITTER AND THE SWEET

With the evolution of modern medicine, the use of such remedies declined. But herbs still serve mankind in a prodigious number of ways. Many are the sources for modern drugs. Among them are the heart stimulant digitalis from foxglove, tranquilizers from rauwolfia and valerian, and burn ointments from the aloe plant.

The worldwide manufacture of cosmetics, foods and drinks also owes much to herbs. Their fragrant oils are used in making soaps, perfumes and lotions. Rubdown liniments get their heating-soothing action (and "healing" smell) from substances like menthol and thymol originally found in wormwood, mint and thyme. Bitter wormwood also flavors alcoholic drinks like vermouth and absinthe although it is poisonous in concentrated form, anise seeds impart their licorice taste to anisette, caraway goes into kümmel, mint makes crème de menthe and angelica helps to flavor gin.

Above all, herbs still go into food. Thousands of tons of them, raised today on farms from California to southern France, lend their flavors to nearly everything we eat: sausages, frankfurters and other processed meats; buns, cookies, crackers and confections; and—in flavors and mixtures to tingle the most jaded palates—every mustard, ketchup, relish, chutney, pickle, mayonnaise, meat sauce, tenderizer and condiment on the supermarket shelf.

Not to mention those bottles of dried stuff in your kitchen—the seeds and leaves from which great herb gardeners often grow.

Beds of flavor and fragrance 2

Centuries ago, when Columbus and other mariners of Genoa were making the city a renowned seaport, many of its sailors relied on their noses to tell them they were near home, for long before they saw land they could smell the thyme blanketing their native Ligurian hills. Liguria, like the other headlands of the Mediterranean, was the home not only of accomplished seamen, but of thyme, rosemary and many of the other plants classified as herbs. They evolved in this sun-warmed, rocky environment, and that fact tells much about the growing conditions they need: sunshine, moisture and well-drained soil.

Not that herbs are fussy. Most grow nearly anyplace that is sunny and not too wet. And even these requirements are not essential for all herbs. Some, mint and parsley among them, tolerate partial shade, and shade is best for woodland herbs like sweet woodruff. But for most of the most popular herbs used today, at least five hours of direct sunlight a day is required, and the availability of sun should determine a herb garden's location. If you have space for a sunny, south-facing bed near the kitchen door you will be twice blessed; you can plant your herb garden there, just a few steps away whenever you need a few flavorful sprigs of tarragon or thyme. Otherwise place your herbs in or alongside a vegetable garden, in pots on a sunny patio, along a garden path or even bordering the front walk. Herbs can be decorative as well as edible if they are arranged with foliage patterns and colors in mind, and they serve admirably as borders, ground covers or accents tucked into odd spaces in a rock garden or between terrace flagstones. Avoid placing them near a good-sized tree, however, and not only because of the shade; shallow, far-reaching tree roots make digging difficult and soon infiltrate among the herbs, robbing them of nutrients and moisture.

Just as important as sunlight is soil with proper drainage; only

A honeybee feasts on the pollen-laden pompons of a chive plant. Ordinarily grown as a flavoring for food, it is one of several herbs with blossoms so decorative they warrant a place as garden ornaments.

a few herbs like sweet flag, sweet woodruff and horseradish can survive having moist soil around their roots for long. The ideal location will be found in a porous, slightly sandy soil or on a gentle slope; any low place where rain water collects and does not drain away quickly should be suspect. If you are not sure that the drainage is adequate at a potential garden site, dig a hole 18 inches wide and equally deep, and fill it with water; if any water is still visible in the hole an hour later, look for another location. If there is no better place that also has sun, do not despair. You can improve the drainage by digging down, as described on page 29, or building up, as shown on page 30.

LAYING OUT THE BED   A simple rectangular plot is the easiest to plant and maintain. It is also the easiest to make into a raised bed, a useful device in any garden and an especially valuable one with herbs. A rectangular plot can be readily divided into rows or beds to suit herbs with various growing habits and requirements. But plan the layout before you set in any plants. It is important to separate perennial herbs from annuals, so that you will not tramp on the perennials when you prepare the soil and plant annuals each year. A plan also will make it easier to allocate shade to shade-tolerant herbs, and to isolate such rampant growers as mint and bee balm, which are apt to spread and pop up among other herbs. Within individual beds you can measure, before planting, the space each kind of herb will require when fully grown. You can also arrange plants according to their respective heights at maturity, placing taller ones like dill, fennel and lovage toward the north side of the bed so they do not shade the shorter species such as parsley or chives to the south.

If all of this planning strikes you as forbidding, consider the kind of helpful guidance that was given the herb gardeners of old. In ancient Rome, Pliny based much of his horticultural advice on his belief in the existence of strong friendships and enmities among plants. Rue dislikes basil, he proclaimed, and hyssop simply cannot get along with the radish. But savory is a good friend of the onion, and the most sociable gathering of all is a bed full of those extroverts, coriander, dill, mallow and chervil.

In medieval times, the superstitions took a darker turn. Those who had trouble growing parsley were told they were too good for it, since parsley would thrive only for the wicked. To overcome his natural goodness, the herb gardener was directed to plant parsley seeds on Good Friday by the light of a rising moon—and furthermore, to plant four times as much as he would need, since parsley had to make nine trips to the devil before it could come up out of the ground. (As is noted elsewhere in this book, parsley *is* extremely slow to germinate.)

Consider working convenience when establishing the dimensions of your herb garden. A single rectangular bed bordering a sunny side of the house can be as wide as three feet and still keep all plants within reach. If you have access to two sides, a bed five feet wide can be comfortably tended. A single bed five feet square provides a modest start, but place it so you will have the option of adding a similar second bed in front of it or to one side, separated by a path two feet wide. In time you may want four beds forming a square with intervening paths. For a more formal, geometrical appearance, this basic pattern can be varied in a number of ways. One of the simplest is to move the corner beds out by a foot or two and notch their inner corners to allow room for a small centerpiece bed as a focal point. Yet another attractive alternative is called a goosefoot design, in which the paths radiate like the rays of the sun from one corner of a square bed.

When you have chosen a location and a design for your herb garden, mark its outlines with lengths of string tied to stakes. Now you are ready to start preparing the beds—in a way that will help your herbs to grow best.

One of the most misleading statements made about herbs is that they thrive in poor soil. To be sure, some, such as thyme and rosemary, cling tenaciously to meager, rocky crevices along their native Mediterranean coastline, while others seem to become less fragrant if, to encourage foliage growth, they are fed a nitrogen-rich

PATTERNS THAT SAVE WORK

fertilizer. But while herbs are less demanding than the hybrids of the rose or vegetable garden, they will not do well in really poor soil. Under such impoverished conditions they will grow a few spindly inches and then go on strike.

As a general rule, herbs thrive in loose soil that is enriched with a moderate amount of organic matter or fertilizer to supply nutrients, and that is close to neutral on the acid-alkaline pH scale. Almost any soil will benefit from the addition of up to one-third organic matter like peat moss or compost, well mixed to the depth of a spading fork, or deeper; it will add body to a light, sandy soil so that it will hold more moisture and nutrients near the roots of the plants, and it will also loosen up a heavy clay soil so that water and air can penetrate more easily. Peat moss has little nutritive value, and unless the soil is already fertile it should be supplemented with a fertilizer such as well-rotted manure, which will also help to lighten the soil. Manure is available in dry bagged form at most local garden centers.

If you use compost, nutrients as well as body will be supplied. You can make rich compost from garden waste. You will need a fence to contain the mix while it brews; drive three or four 4-foot

THREE CONCRETE-BLOCK MINIGARDENS

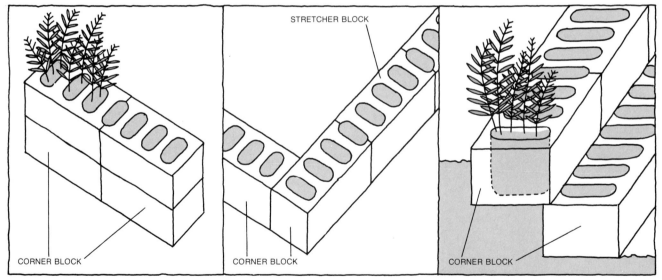

For a simple herb planter, stack masonry corner blocks one atop another. Fill the cores of the lower tier with pebbles for drainage, cover with aluminum or plastic screening and fill the upper cores with soil. Then plant herbs.

To form an herb border, use a combination of corner blocks and stretcher blocks (blocks with half cores at both ends). Set the blocks directly on the ground, or dig a trench and bury them halfway. Fill the cores with soil and plant.

To make tiers for a gentle incline, stack overlapping blocks. Starting at the bottom of the slope and working on one level at a time, dig a shallow trench and sink the blocks into it. Make no more than three tiers, and overlap the blocks an inch or so.

stakes a foot into the ground and wrap small-mesh wire fencing around them to form an enclosure 3 feet high. Inside it, blend dead leaves, grass clippings, weeds, and other vegetable matter like beet or carrot tops. On top of each 4- to 6-inch layer of this organic material, sprinkle three or four handfuls of a high-nitrogen garden fertilizer like 10-10-10, a mixture of compounds providing 10 per cent nitrogen, 10 per cent phosphorus and 10 per cent potassium. The strong nitrogen content is beneficial because it feeds the bacteria that break down the raw organic material into rich, brown compost; the high proportion of phosphorus is important in building strong roots and stems, and the potassium helps the perennial herbs to resist winter cold. Add a dusting of ground limestone to reduce acidity, and blanket each layer with a couple of inches of soil to speed the heat-decay process inside. Make the top slightly concave so that it will catch rain, keep the pile moist and turn it over every month or six weeks. In six months or less you will have a dark, crumbly, well-rotted mixture ideal as an organic additive for preparing your herb beds, and for refreshing them in subsequent growing seasons.

To make sure your soil has the right chemistry for the herbs you are planting, test it before preparing the beds. You can determine the acidity or alkalinity—pH—of your soil with a kit sold at many garden centers, or by sending a soil sample to your local agricultural extension service for analysis. Most herbs will do well in a range of 6.0 to 7.5, measured on a scale that runs from 0 at the acid end through 7 for neutral to 14 at the alkaline end. If your soil is too acid for the herbs you plan to grow, work 5 pounds of finely ground limestone into each 100 square feet of planting area to raise the pH ½ to 1 point. If the soil is too alkaline, use ½ pound of ground sulfur, or 3 pounds of iron sulfate or aluminum sulfate, to lower the pH an equal amount; the ground sulfur is slower acting but its effect on the soil lasts longer.

MODIFYING SOIL CHEMISTRY

If you have soil with exceptionally poor drainage, say with an impermeable layer of hardpan beneath the surface, you may be able to improve it by installing a percolation layer. Dig down a good foot or more, setting aside clumps of sod, dark topsoil and lighter subsoil in separate heaps. In the bottom of the excavated bed, spread a 3-inch layer of heavy gravel or crushed rock. Make a layer of the sod clumps on top of it, then add some of the subsoil, generously mixed with sand. Finally, cover the bed with the topsoil mixed with compost or peat moss and any other necessary additives required by the herbs.

An easier way to assure good drainage for the herb beds is to raise them at least partly above ground level. A raised bed is an old tradition in herb gardening—in fact it was called a "bed" because it looked like one designed for sleeping in. Almost regardless of the kind of soil below it, a raised bed guarantees the drainage these plants need. Excess water will trickle down at least to ground level and drain away. The elevated soil will also become dry and warm somewhat earlier in the spring, often allowing planting days ahead of the surrounding ground-level soil.

There are other good reasons for constructing raised planting areas in an herb garden. They keep the garden neater, providing well-defined places for planting and holding everything in its place.

A BEGINNER'S GARDEN

1. *The 3-by-6-foot herb garden diagramed at right is raised for easy access. Vary the dimensions as required, but keep the width to 3 feet or less for easy access to all plants. Construct the frame from 1-by-8-inch lumber, protecting it with copper naphthenate stain. Assemble the frame with galvanized spikes or angle brackets.*

2. *Remove sod from an area the size of the frame in a location that receives at least six hours of sun daily. Dig over the soil, removing any roots or rubble. Work in 2 inches of compost or 3 inches of peat moss, ½ pound of 5-10-5 fertilizer for every 10 square feet, and limestone or sulfur to correct the pH factor (page 29). Dig a 3-inch-deep trench around the plot and lower the frame into it. Spade in enough topsoil to fill comfortably; you will need about ten 50-pound bags.*

3. *Select the herbs you wish to plant, or start with the following basic herbs, which should fill the needs of a family of four: six parsley plants, one large clump (or two small ones) of chives, six plants each of basil and dill, one each of sage, oregano, tarragon, thyme and rosemary, and three mint plants— one each of spearmint, peppermint, and lemon or orange mint.*

Annuals can be planted each year in one raised bed, while perennials can remain undisturbed in another. Within beds, plants that naturally have a tidy appearance, like lavender cotton or germander, can be used along the edges, with more unruly growers like horseradish and wormwood set behind them. Free-ranging plants such as the mints can be grown in their own separate beds, whose sides will block and contain their invasive roots. Similarly, the raised sides stop grass and other ground covers from moving in, and the gravel or wood chips of garden paths are not scuffed in among the plants. Nor do you need to bend over quite so far when you weed or harvest the herbs.

RAISED BEDS

Above ground beds pay esthetic dividends, too. The geometrical pattern of the garden, emphasized by the three-dimensional look of the raised edges, is pleasing to the eye, and such a garden looks orderly and attractive at any time of year, whether it is full of growing plants or not. If the beds are raised a foot or more, you can widen their edges to provide benches where you can sit while you enjoy the fragrance.

Almost any kind of container can be used to make a raised bed for herbs—a long planter box, a rock retaining wall, even hollow concrete building blocks or flue tiles filled with soil.

Higher beds can be edged with boards 2 inches thick and 10 or 12 inches wide, held together with angle irons. Heavy timbers or railroad ties, which make durable frames for raised beds, can be laid on the surface of the ground and held in position with stakes.

EDGING THAT LASTS

Rotproof edging can be built with stones, rectangular pieces of slate set on edge, or strips of asbestos building board cut to order with a special saw. One of the simplest permanent edgings, both attractive and traditional, is made with plain bricks either set on end in a shallow trench or laid horizontally two or three courses high. For a simple and inexpensive bed, use 1- by 8-inch boards. Boards of whatever size should be protected against rot with two coats of copper naphthenate stain (which comes in several colors). Avoid creosote or pentachlorophenol wood preservatives; they are toxic to plants. As you spade to prepare the soil in the beds, sink the boards around the edges 2 or 3 inches below ground level to keep them in place, leaving the remainder of the width extending above the ground. Finish preparing the soil inside, mixing in any necessary nutrients and organic matter and adding extra soil if necessary, so the soil surface is about an inch below the top.

Most of this preparatory work is best done a season in advance. Since additives like limestone and sulfur do not take full effect for months, it is a good idea to incorporate them into the beds in the fall for spring planting or in the spring for fall planting. Preparing your beds ahead also allows time for organic additives like compost or manure to blend into the soil in a form most usable to the plants, and it gives the beds time to settle naturally under rainfall to their permanent level before the planting season arrives.

If you live in Zones 3–7 *(map, page 150)*, you should be ready to plant herbs soon after frost leaves the ground in spring; in Zones 8–10, you can plant at virtually any time of year, although many gardeners favor fall planting because the relatively cool season ahead permits the plants to become well established before the arrival of hot summer weather. Wait until the soil has dried enough to be crumbly when spaded, then turn over once more, to the depth of a spading fork, the settled beds you prepared some months earlier. Break up clods of earth with the back of the spading fork, and rake out any loose stones that turn up. If the soil is still a little too heavy or too light, or if you are renewing beds used the

TRANSPLANTING SEEDLINGS

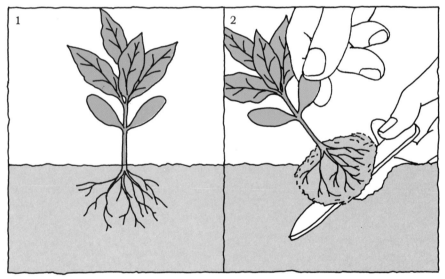

Separate and transplant seedlings grown in pots or seedbeds when they are about 2 inches tall and after they have produced two pairs of true leaves above the rounded pair of seed leaves. Moisten the soil sufficiently to permit easy separation of the seedlings with minimum disturbance to their roots.

Gently grasp one of the rounded seed leaves—never hold a young plant by its delicate stem—and use the pointed end of a plant marker to pry up the roots. Still holding the plant by a seed leaf, carefully lift the seedling out of the ground. To minimize transplanting shock, replant the herb immediately.

previous year, dig in an additional inch of compost or 2 or 3 inches of peat moss. If the soil lacks nutrients, dig in a quick-acting balanced chemical fertilizer. The best choice for most herbs is 5-10-5. Mix the fertilizer into the soil at a rate of 3 to 4 pounds per 100 square feet. If your soil needs only phosphorus, you can substitute 3 to 6 pounds of bone meal per 100 square feet. Or if only potassium is called for, you can supply all that most herbs need with a scattering of wood ashes from a fireplace.

Most herbs can be bought in the form of young plants ready to set out in the garden, but you may choose to raise annuals from seed. Sow them directly outdoors as soon as the ground can be prepared. A simple way to space plants properly is to mark off a grid by pressing a hoe handle into the soil at the intervals specified for mature plants; at each intersection of the lines thus made, sprinkle a few seeds and cover them with a little soil.

STARTING FROM SCRATCH

A rule of thumb is to cover seeds to a depth equal to two or three times their diameter; tiny seeds like those of thyme are simply dropped on the surface of the loose soil to work their way in. Press down the soil around the seeds with the heel of your hand to firm it into little saucer-like depressions, which will gather water. The depressions will also mark the places where you should be careful about weeding until the seedling herbs can be identified. Moisten the bed with a fine spray from a garden hose and keep it moist but not soggy until the seedlings sprout. Burlap or loose-mesh cheesecloth, laid temporarily over the beds and anchored with stones, will hold moisture in sunny or windy gardens and will keep heavy rain from washing seeds away; just make sure that you remove the covering as soon as the seedlings sprout.

When the seedlings are about 2 inches high or have developed their first pairs of true leaves (recognizable as those of the species), snip off all but the strongest plant in each cluster—and eat the discards as the first tender taste of your garden herbs.

THINNING TO TASTE

Many gardeners make two or three sowings of herbs like dill and fennel at 10-day to three-week intervals until early summer, to extend the season when fresh crops of leaves or seeds will be available for picking.

Seeds of some herbs—annuals like dill and borage as well as perennials like thyme and hyssop—can also be sown in late fall after warm weather is past. They will remain dormant over winter and come up the following spring.

For a head start with the seeds of slow-growing perennials like winter savory and thyme, plant seeds indoors in pots four to six weeks before the last frost is expected *(map, page 151)*. Moisten the soil by standing the container in a tray of water until the surface becomes slightly damp, then plant the seeds. Cover the container with plastic kitchen wrap and set it away from bright light in a place where the temperature will remain between 65° and 75°. When the seeds have sprouted, generally in a week to 15 days (the reluctant parsley may take three weeks), remove the plastic and set the containers on a sunny window sill. Turn them every day to maintain an even growth rate and to keep the seedlings from leaning toward the light. Before the seedlings become crowded, transplant them to individual containers or thin them by clipping off all but the strongest plants in the batch.

MOVING SEEDLINGS To transplant, lift them out of the containers one by one, using a plant marker or tongue depressor to pry up the root system of each with a little ball of soil. Steady the top of the plant with a gentle hold on a leaf—never touch the tender stem—and lower the root ball into a prepared hole. You can transplant seedlings into compartmentalized plastic trays, clay or plastic pots or peat pots; in the latter case, the peat pots are eventually set in the garden with the plants. The roots grow through the sides of the disintegrating peat pots and into the surrounding soil with a minimum amount of transplant shock.

TEMPERING THE SHOCK When the weather has moderated sufficiently, depending on each plant's tolerance for cold as well as your climate zone, firm the seedlings gently into the soil and make a little saucer-like depression around each to catch and hold moisture, setting the plants no deeper than they were growing indoors. Stick identification markers next to the plants and water them with a fine mist from a garden hose. To ease the abrupt change from indoor to outdoor conditions, try to transplant on a mild, overcast day, and shade the tender seedlings for a day or two with cheesecloth held above them on stakes, or with a shingle or a leafy twig pushed into the soil on the south side of the plants. (Nursery-grown plants of sturdier perennials such as tarragon, rosemary or sage, however, do not require such precautions and can be set into the ground at almost any time after they are purchased.)

Once the plants are growing in the garden, make sure they get enough moisture. Never let the soil become completely dry. A common mistake with herbs is to water them too frequently and too shallowly with a fast once-over from the hose. The best rule is not to water unless you can see leaves beginning to wilt. Then water deeply and thoroughly, either spraying patiently and slowly until the soil is moist to a depth of 12 inches or stringing a canvas soaker hose through the plant bed and letting it run for an hour or two.

To shade the soil and thus help it retain moisture, and to smother most weeds before they start, many herb gardeners apply a summer mulch around the plants when they are about 6 inches tall. Wood chips, ground bark, chunky (poultry grade) peat moss, ground corncobs, buckwheat hulls or pine needles will do the job without holding so much moisture that the plants rot. Spread the mulch 1 to 2 inches thick between the plants, tapering off to ½ inch near the stems.

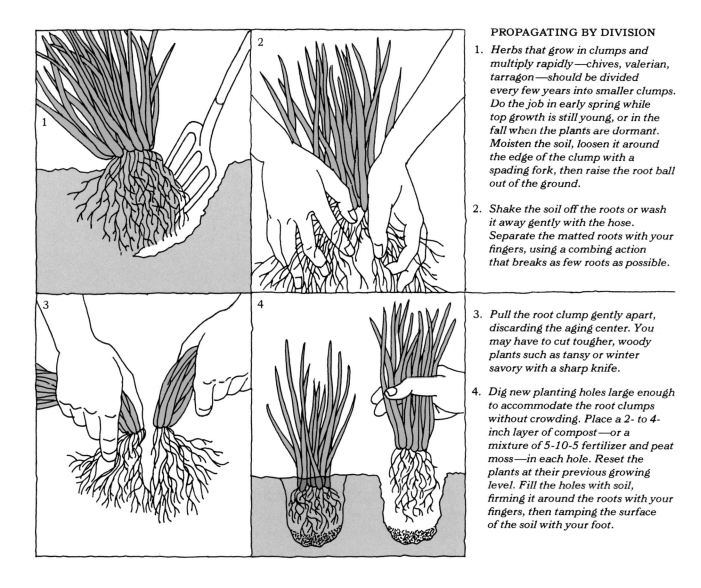

PROPAGATING BY DIVISION

1. *Herbs that grow in clumps and multiply rapidly—chives, valerian, tarragon—should be divided every few years into smaller clumps. Do the job in early spring while top growth is still young, or in the fall when the plants are dormant. Moisten the soil, loosen it around the edge of the clump with a spading fork, then raise the root ball out of the ground.*

2. *Shake the soil off the roots or wash it away gently with the hose. Separate the matted roots with your fingers, using a combing action that breaks as few roots as possible.*

3. *Pull the root clump gently apart, discarding the aging center. You may have to cut tougher, woody plants such as tansy or winter savory with a sharp knife.*

4. *Dig new planting holes large enough to accommodate the root clumps without crowding. Place a 2- to 4-inch layer of compost—or a mixture of 5-10-5 fertilizer and peat moss—in each hole. Reset the plants at their previous growing level. Fill the holes with soil, firming it around the roots with your fingers, then tamping the surface of the soil with your foot.*

That is all the care most herbs need, except for pulling an occasional weed. Some of the larger, faster-growing species—like dill, fennel, lovage and chervil, for instance—will benefit from a scattering of 5-10-5 fertilizer next to them when they are about a foot tall. Few herbs are attacked by diseases, and their fragrant oils, which make them so attractive to humans, seem to repel most insects. Insecticides are seldom necessary, and in any case are best not used on edible herbs. If you do find that insects are nibbling on your herbs, knock them off with a stiff spray from the garden hose.

Once started properly, an herb garden should flourish year after year with a little care—and vigilance—on your part. Many annual and biennial herbs—dill, mustard and caraway, for example—will perpetuate themselves if you allow some of your plants to produce and drop their seeds, though you will have to learn to recognize the tiny wayward seedlings so you can transplant them back to their proper places.

Perennials like chives, tarragon, yarrow and bergamot can be multiplied by division when they become large. In fact, they will be more vigorous as well as more numerous if they are dug up, divided and replanted about every third year. From Zone 6 south, pull or cut such plants apart after they have flowered; from Zone 5 north it is better to divide root clumps in very early spring while they are still dormant, giving the new plants a long growing season to develop strong root systems.

PROPAGATION BY DIVISION   To divide an old plant, dig deeply around it with a spade and lift it out of the ground with as much of the root ball intact as possible; then pull the plant apart with your hands. You may have to cut some of the roots apart with a large knife or a sharp spade. Discard the aging and compacted center section of the clump and place each young outer section in a hole of ample size in a bed that has been spaded to a depth of a foot or more and conditioned with compost, peat moss, and a scattering of 5-10-5 fertilizer. Set the plants at the depth at which they were previously growing and fill in the hole with soil, firming it well with your feet and soaking it with water when you are through.

If you are dividing growing plants in summer or fall, cut their stems halfway back so that their root systems, abbreviated in the process of dividing, will have less top growth to support. If you plan to pot sections of chives or parsley to bring indoors for fresh flavorings in the winter, pot them in late summer but let them sit outdoors for a month or two before moving them to a sunny window sill in the house.

Many perennial herbs—lavender, rosemary, southernwood, lemon balm and others—can be propagated from stem cuttings, a method that leaves the parent plants undisturbed. Stem cuttings can be made in spring or early summer in northern zones, and at any time the plants are in active growth elsewhere. Cut off a 4- to 6-inch tip of a leaf stem, choosing one that is firm but not hardened and woody, and making the cut just below a point where a leaf stalk meets the stem. Strip the lowest leaves from the cutting and pinch off any buds or flowers; dip the bare end into hormone rooting powder (available at most garden centers) and insert each cutting about an inch deep in a pot or tray filled with a well-moistened rooting medium such as vermiculite, perlite, shredded

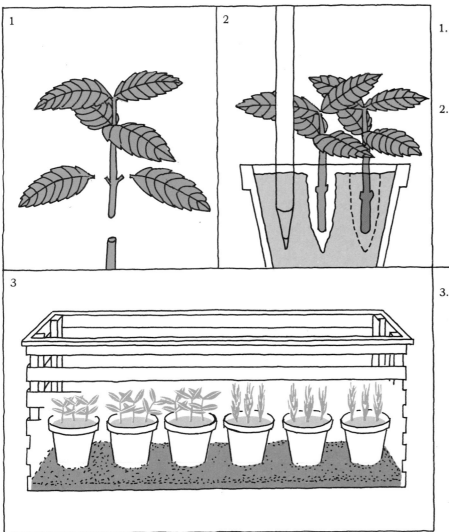

PROPAGATING TIP CUTTINGS

1. *Cut 4- to 6-inch-long young, strong tips, about ¼ inch below a leaf joint. Clip off the lower leaves, leaving an inch or so of bare stem and at least three to five leaves.*

2. *Dip the cut end of each slip into a bit of hormone rooting powder, never directly into the hormone container. Fill 4-inch pots with dampened coarse sand or perlite and pierce with three or four pencil-sized holes deep enough to cover the bare leaf joints. Insert a cutting into each hole, and firm the sand or perlite around it.*

3. *To provide both moisture and air circulation, place the potted cuttings in a slatted box, such as an orange crate, lined on the bottom with a 2-inch layer of damp peat moss or coarse sand. Cover the top of the box with a piece of glass or plastic, and set it outdoors in the shade. When new top growth appears, transplant the cuttings into individual pots filled with commercial potting soil, firming the soil around the new roots. Set the plants in the garden when you can see a network of new white roots in the soil ball when you tap a plant from its pot.*

sphagnum moss or builder's sand. Enclose the pot or tray in a clear plastic food bag or plastic kitchen wrap to conserve moisture, inserting plant markers or pencils in the medium to prop the plastic above the leaves. Tuck the open end of the plastic under the container, set this miniature greenhouse in a bright location out of direct sun, and make sure the rooting medium stays moist.

When the cuttings develop small new leaves, generally in two to four weeks, and their roots are about 1 inch long (gently pry one up to look), move them to separate pots filled with packaged potting soil. After two or three weeks tap one out of the pot to examine the root system. When the roots are strong enough, the herbs can be planted in the garden at least in warmer climates. In cold regions they can be transplanted into individual pots filled with commercial potting soil and held indoors over winter to be set in the garden the following spring.

Cuttings made from roots rather than stems can be taken from plants that send up new stems from spreading roots—Aaron's rod, bee balm, horehound and perennial species of sage among others. Slice off the outer ends of a few roots with a sharp spade, discard the tapering thin ends of the roots and cut the remainders into sections 1 to 2 inches long. Lay these sections flat in a tray or box an inch or so apart on top of 3 inches of builder's sand or light garden soil, then cover them with ½ inch of the growing medium and water them thoroughly.

In cooler regions root cuttings are best made in the fall and stored in the same growing medium on a cool porch or in a cold frame outdoors until they send up shoots in spring and can be planted in the garden. In warmer climates the tray or box can simply be covered with plastic wrap or a plastic food bag and set outdoors out of direct sun; when new growth appears, the covering should be removed. When the new plants are 2 to 3 inches high they are ready for the garden.

For shrubby perennial herbs like jasmine and rose, whose long, flexible stems sometimes droop along the ground, the ground-layering method of starting new plants is convenient. In northern zones this technique is best used in early spring to give the new plants time to establish themselves in the garden before frost. Bend a stem down so it touches the ground about a foot from its tip. At this point scrape the lower surface with a knife if the stem is slender; in a thicker stem make a slanting cut partway through the underside and wedge the cut open with a matchstick. Dust the exposed surface with hormone rooting powder, then bend the treated section down into a shallow dish-shaped hole lined with a mix-

AN HERB BRED FOR FLAVOR AND LOOKS

The development in 1962 of a new variety of basil, dubbed Dark Opal for its deep purple leaves, marked a milestone in the age-old history of herbs—a category of plants seldom subjected to the intensive breeding lavished on other members of the horticultural kingdom. Perfected at the University of Connecticut, utilizing a purple-tinged basil native to Turkey, Dark Opal is one of the few man-made herbs and the only herb ever to win the All-America medal awarded by professional seedsmen. This award, the equivalent to seed developers of the Oscar to motion-picture professionals, is given by a jury of experts to a select group of new plants that meet the jury's standards of excellence for that year. Traditionally handed out to glamorous flowering plants—marigolds, zinnias and snapdragons have been frequent winners—the medal was bestowed on Dark Opal basil for its ornamental qualities, specifically for its shiny, wine-dark leaves and its two-toned lavender-and-white blossoms. But Dark Opal is also useful, and its leaves can be snipped into foods whenever basil is called for.

ture of equal parts of soil, peat moss and coarse builder's sand. Pin the section down with a loop of wire and bury it in more soil mix, leaving about 6 inches of the stem tip protruding. Soak the buried section with water and put a stone on top to hold and mark the stem. Nourished by the parent plant, it may sprout roots of its own in as little as six weeks.

When the roots are established, as indicated by new growth on the exposed tip, cut the stem from its parent just below the ball of soil formed by the new roots. Transplant the new herb to a place of its own in the garden.

To get the most from your herb garden, practice a few simple procedures to prolong the life of existing plants. Unless you find the flowers particularly decorative, pinch off the flower buds of basil, summer savory and other annuals and biennials; disbudding will delay their blossoming so you can harvest fresh leaves that much longer through the summer.

ROUTINE MAINTENANCE

To keep perennial herbs healthy through the winter, they should be given some special attention in the fall. When the leaves of plants like sage and chives have withered, cut the old stalks to the ground. Move tender evergreen perennials like rosemary inside before the frosts arrive.

After the ground has frozen hard—and not before—guard perennial beds against premature thaws. They will be much better off if they remain frozen all winter long and are not subjected to alternate thawing and freezing, which can push plants out of the ground and cause serious damage to the roots. This protection is provided by a winter mulch; like a summer mulch, it is a blanket against the sun—to keep plants cold, not warm. It must be light and porous enough to allow air to penetrate, yet thick enough to shade and insulate the soil.

WINTER PROTECTION

A winter mulch can be made of crisscrossed evergreen boughs such as those left over from Christmas trees, or of a thick blanket of pine needles or straw. The most satisfactory, however, is salt or marsh hay. Unlike ordinary hay, it is springy and relatively nonabsorbent, so it does not mat down when it gets wet; and it is less likely than ordinary hay to introduce weeds, since the seeds it contains will sprout only in their natural habitat of salty mud flats, not in garden soil. If you can get some, buy a bale or two and spread it in a 4- to 6-inch layer over your perennial herb beds. Remove the mulch when the first new sprouts of your herbs come up to greet the warmth of another spring.

Displays of beauty from utilitarian plants

Herb gardens started out as—and in most places still are—humbly practical affairs: small plots hard by the kitchen door for the prudent housewife to reach into when she needed sprigs to flavor her stews or treat her family's ills. But in the 16th Century these once-prosaic gardens became high fashion. Noblemen ordered the construction of conceits like knot gardens *(right),* in which the utilitarian herbs were planted and pruned in elaborate patterns. Although few homeowners bother with such extravagances today, herbs are gaining renewed popularity, and modern gardeners find both traditional and innovative ways of using them decoratively.

To be a success, an herb garden must take into account the way herbs are used as well as their special physical qualities. Few bear spectacular blossoms. Yet the very lack of ostentatious flowers gives prominence to the subtle variations of color, texture and shape of their foliage. Equally important are their growth habits. Many herbs are tenaciously unruly. They sprawl above ground and spread below ground, leading many herbalists to impose order on the rambunctious plants by laying them out in geometric designs.

Most experts recommend that an herb garden be enclosed, if only by a low hedge. Besides providing shelter from the wind, an enclosure lends a formal structure to the garden. A central focal point—a special plant, a garden ornament, a small pool—serves the same purpose. Given these design elements, a patterned layout of planting beds seems both natural and logical. For ease in tending and harvesting the herbs, the beds are often raised. This arrangement also improves drainage—a necessity for most herbs—and it allows greater flexibility. In many gardens the plants themselves are divided into beds according to leaf color, height, use or growing habits. But gardeners seeking a more informal look plant their beds with mixtures of herbs and create visual unity with edgings of bricks or of a single perennial herb. Paths between the beds help to contain and frame the herbs while allowing access to the garden. Used together or singly, in small scale or large, these ideas lead to an herb garden that is tidy and handsome all year round.

A knot garden at the Brooklyn Botanic Garden displays herbs simulating intertwined strands.

Common herbs uncommonly employed

A low dense hedge of gray-green santolina outlines the edge of a swimming pool in suburban Philadelphia. This linear herb garden not only perfumes the air but serves as a barrier, protecting the pool from drifting leaves carried by the wind from the adjacent lawn. To encourage bushy growth, the hedge must be clipped hard twice a year—in early spring and midsummer—with a few touch-ups in between.

The family dog and a "topiary" bird— created by shaping two myrtle bushes—face off on a Pennsylvania lawn. The owner shaped the bird from a piece of heavy galvanized wire staked between two container-grown plants (they must be taken indoors in winter). As branches grew, supported by the wire, they were bent to form the tail, then the back and head, and finally trimmed into the bird shape.

Myrtle coils 5 ½ feet high, sculpted by the topiarist who created the bird opposite, are made from bushes supported by stakes.

An order established by geometry

Angular beds edged in brick and raised above a background of white gravel walks establish and maintain the pattern of this terraced herb garden. On the upper level, triangular beds of yarrow, lady's mantle, sorrel and rosemary are set off by a large rectangular bed devoted entirely to mint. The round bed on the lower level contains lemon thyme, while lavender and germander fill the two wedges in front of the bench. The two tall-growing herbs that tower above all other plants in the garden are mullein.

A brick-edged wheel 15 feet across is divided into wedges, each of which is a unique environment, dry or moist, acid or alkaline. One, at lower right, contains woad, madder and Nepal cinquefoil—all ancient dye plants suited to a dry, mild climate. An orange tree shades the south quadrant, for herbs that cannot stand full sun.

Cinder blocks form the individual beds in this bushy green herb garden tended by volunteers at the Botanical Garden of the University of North Carolina. Typical is the center bed, with mounds of gray santolina surrounded by germander and framed at the edge by two species of thyme. The one touch of red (far right) is blossoming bee balm.

Two adjoining rectangular beds raised on concrete footings and edged with native fieldstone frame this herb garden in Ithaca, New York. Slate benches built into the bed invite sitting—a particularly pleasant idea for a garden devoted to fragrant herbs. Among its plantings are five kinds of thyme, two of sage and two clumps of lavender in full bloom. The spikey flowers at the rear of the first bed are foxglove; the fragile blossoms of the plant in the foreground of the second bed are horehound.

Dooryard gardens for use and show

Into a tiny back-door herb garden in Connecticut (left) the owner has incorporated such culinary or scented herbs as rosemary, lavender, artemisia, thyme, parsley, winter savory and horseradish, plus a few non-herbs like shasta daisies and a pear tree.

A weathered picket fence hems in a cornucopia of herbs outside a Connecticut farmhouse, above. Enclosed in a compact accessible space are some 16 culinary herbs from angelica to thyme, along with a few, like lavender and southernwood, grown for color and aroma.

Just off a terrace, and overlooked by the living room windows, a colorful herb garden in suburban Philadelphia was designed for year-round viewing. A low brick wall encloses it, and the flagstone walks that meander through it are bordered with woolly lamb's ears, an herb that keeps its silvery foliage all winter. So do the dark green dwarf boxwoods that punctuate the garden at intervals. Along with such herbs as hyssop, thyme, sage, lavender and lady's mantle are a few non-herbs—begonias, pygmy barberry, a tree peony—for added visual interest.

The essential pathways

A wide gravel walk edged with cedar planks gives easy access to a garden near the sea in Mystic, Connecticut. The plot is 20 feet square, surrounded on three sides with a post-and-rail fence, on the fourth by bricks and a hedge of lavender. Included in this mixture of annual and perennial herbs are some in pots—such as the sweet bay at the near inner right hand corner of the walk—that are taken indoors for the winter.

Wood chips cover two intersecting paths that cut through a broad expanse of woodruff on the grounds of a Pennsylvania home. Woodruff, the crucial flavoring for May wine, is one of the few herbs that grow in the shade. Here it is used as a ground cover underneath trees. The tidy paths are appropriate to the woodland setting and permit strollers to enjoy the plant's glossy leaves and tiny star-shaped flowers at close range.

A broad grassy path edged in brick bisects a varied herb garden outside Philadelphia. The bricks, which separate the path from the garden, also disguise an even more effective boundary. Beneath them lies a three-foot-deep trench, filled with concrete, that curbs aggressive roots. The herbs in the garden include Chinese chives in the left foreground and, midway down the right border, a tall clump of basil.

Brick paths weave through a rambling herb and flower garden set in the middle of the Connecticut countryside, bringing a sense of order to an otherwise informal and rustic design. Rosemary, savory, sage, thyme, betony, agrimony and yarrow—to name but a few of the plants—intermingle with delphiniums, moss roses, a quince tree and a pear tree. The flowering border is of yellow chamomile and orange marigolds.

Mirrors of the past

Four gates in a prim picket fence open into a large herb
garden at Pennsbury, the restoration of William Penn's home
near Morrisville, Pennsylvania. Penn, like many prudent
colonists, grew his own herbs for household use—his first wife's
recipe collection contains many references to them. The exact
composition and location of Penn's garden have been lost, but this
reconstruction, typical of 17th Century herb gardens, is
thought to be much like his. Among the luxuriant plantings in the
foreground are plots of tarragon, left, with horehound behind
it; rue in the center; and a clump of basil in full flower, right,
behind dark green hyssop.

An early 18th Century limestone wall and a sculptured yew
hedge enclose the herb garden at Cranborne Manor in Dorset,
England, right, re-created by its present owner, Lady Salisbury,
on what is thought to be the site of the manor's original 13th
Century herb garden. Between 150 and 200 varieties of herbs are
contained in the garden—scented, culinary and medicinal—
including a number of very old species, such as English mace,
pennyroyal and motherwort. There are also between 15 and
20 kinds of thyme, as well as many marjorams, sages and mints.

A garden on the window sill 3

The apartment of a young computer programer in a Chicago high-rise is an island of aromatic greenery in a sea of sterile concrete. Outside her windows is the city, indoors are pots, baskets and trays of growing herbs. In the living room a sweet olive, its stems laden with tiny chartreuse blooms, blends its fragrance with that of a snowy jasmine. In the kitchen this accomplished gardener snips sprigs of orange mint and thyme to add to celery leaves in a soup bag which she drops into a steaming kettle of fresh green pea soup, transforming it from a plebeian to an epicurean dish. She raises herbs not just for their looks and aroma but for the extra flavor only home-grown, freshly cut seasonings can give; anyone who dines at her table can tell the difference.

The profusion of plants, bushy and vigorous, thriving in that environment so distant from a garden makes it seem that herbs grow readily indoors. They do, if like the young Chicago computer programer, you know how to encourage them.

Some experienced gardeners will tell you that growing herbs indoors is child's play, and in view of all the herb-growing kits on the market and the number of pots to be seen flourishing on kitchen window sills, you might take them at their word. But other gardeners, equally skilled, will tell you that herbs are the most recalcitrant of house plants. Both are partly right.

A comfortably large number of plants classified as herbs—including such culinary favorites as basil, bay, parsley and tarragon, and such tropical, subtropical and desert plants as scented geraniums, jasmine, sweet olive and aloe—grow readily indoors. But, like all plants, their demands must be met if they are to prosper. Most should have at least five hours of direct sunlight a day, night temperatures under 60°, good drainage, and high humidity as in a steamy kitchen. Given these conditions, they will reward you with a year-round supply of flavorings and unusual greenery.

Safe from frost and handy for snipping, bushy thyme, broad-leaved basil and tall-growing sage thrive in one pot on a sunny window sill beside a pot of peppermint geranium. Nearby hang stalks of dried dill.

Many apartment dwellers have no place for an outdoor garden, yet they enjoy having a pot or two of each of their favorite herbs indoors the year round. Outdoor gardeners in cold climates often bring some herbs indoors in the fall so they can continue to harvest them through the winter, particularly those like chives and parsley that taste so much better fresh than frozen or dried. Or they may move in tender shrubby herbs like rosemary, sweet bay and lemon verbena that would not survive freezing. Indoor herb gardening also provides a chance to try plants that in northern zones will prosper only in controlled warmth and moisture.

In selecting herbs to grow indoors, it is well to follow a few rules. The first involves size. Most herbs grow smaller indoors because they get less than ideal light, temperature and room for their roots. Nevertheless, unless you have a great deal of space you will probably want to avoid large plants like angelica, which grows 5 feet tall or more in the garden and half that size indoors, as well as sprawling plants like lady's mantle or cardoon. Smaller and more compact species like sweet marjoram, thyme, parsley, winter sa-

HERBS THAT HANG

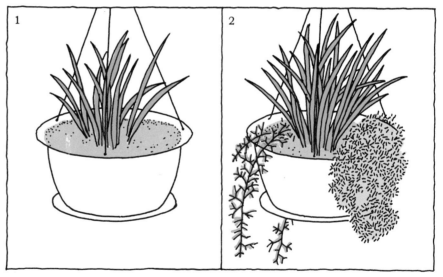

Select a plastic hanging pot that is equipped with an attached saucer to prevent dripping. Fill the pot with commercial potting soil and plant upright-growing herbs such as chives, basil or parsley in the center. Start with well-rooted plants so that the ultimate space requirements for the full-grown root balls of the various plants can be properly gauged.

Choose prostrate or cascading herbs such as lemon verbena, trailing rosemary, creeping thyme or nasturtium to plant around the outer edge of the garden. Hang the pot in a sunny window, and snip off ends of the herbs frequently to keep the foliage growing abundantly and to control the size and shape of the separate plants.

vory and chives not only allow you to have more plants and greater variety, but they blend better with the smaller scale of indoor surroundings. Few houses or apartments have space for plants like anise, coriander and caraway that are grown primarily for their seeds; to get enough seeds to be practical you would need several of each. Finally, some herbs simply are not suited to indoor growing—horseradish, orris root and marsh mallow among them—and unless you like challenges you will give them low priority.

The herbs you select to grow indoors are propagated like those raised in the garden. Plants that can be grown easily from seed—basil, dill, lavender, nasturtium and parsley, for example—can be sown in pots 3 to 6 inches in diameter any time in late summer. Start the seedlings outside if you have a place to do so, preferably six to 10 weeks before the first frosts are expected in your area, so that they will be growing vigorously when they have to face the adjustment of being moved inside. Sow three or four seeds in each pot, keep them barely moist and in a shady spot until they germinate, then move them into sunlight. When the seedlings are an inch or two tall, thin them to save the single healthiest-looking one in each pot. Move the pots inside before the first frost is expected.

Perennials like thyme, mint, chives and lemon balm can be potted up from plants growing in the garden or bought from a nursery in late summer. If you are taking plants from the garden, dig up the entire plant at least a month before expected frosts. You can divide a large plant into several of more manageable size (*Chapter 2*). Set each plant into a pot that is about 1 inch larger than the ball of soil around the roots. Usually a pot 4 or 5 inches in diameter will suffice. Cut back a third to a half of the top growth to compensate for roots damaged in digging, keep the plants in shade for a week or 10 days to give them a chance to recover, then gradually move them into full sun until time to take them indoors. Cut off worn-out foliage at the soil level to encourage vigorous new growth. Plants can also be started by means of stem cuttings, root cuttings or ground layering, as described in Chapter 2.

When buying plants, look for stocky, bushy ones with plenty of rich green (not pale or brown-edged) lower leaves. Check the soil surface in the pot and the drainage hole in the bottom; if roots are beginning to protrude either above or below, the plant may need repotting, a job you should do before bringing it indoors. It is also a good idea to check the stems and undersides of leaves for insect infestations. Although herbs are relatively pest free, they sometimes pick up pests from other plants; watch out for the speckled

PLANT TOWER FOR A PATIO

1. *To grow herbs in a small area such as a balcony, patio or deck, construct a cylindrical herb tower from a 4-foot-wide piece of 3-inch welded wire mesh, cut to measure 5 feet long. Do not use chicken wire—the small openings make planting difficult.*

2. *Position in the mesh rectangle so the long sides are parallel to the floor, and carefully bend it into a cylinder. Twist the cut ends of wire around a vertical section of the mesh to hold the structure together, turning the tips inward.*

3. *Line the cylinder with waterproof kraft building paper. For a movable tower, mount it on a 2-foot square of ¾-inch exterior plywood fitted with casters. For a stationary one, put a circular piece of lining material under it. Fill the cylinder with commercial potting soil.*

4. *Mark squares for planting holes, staggering them so that one is not directly beneath another. Leave enough closed squares to support the soil. Using a sharp knife, cut out the liner at the marked squares.*

5. *Select the herbs you wish to plant. Position upright herbs such as chives or basil at the top and spreading ones such as mint at the bottom. Moisture-loving plants should also be located at the bottom. Set plants at a slight angle in the cutout holes, or plant seeds, three or four to a hole, at a depth three times their diameter.*

6. *When the tower is completely planted, water it thoroughly from the top. Make sure the garden is kept constantly moist, watering it daily in dry weather, or using a hose attachment that drips water.*

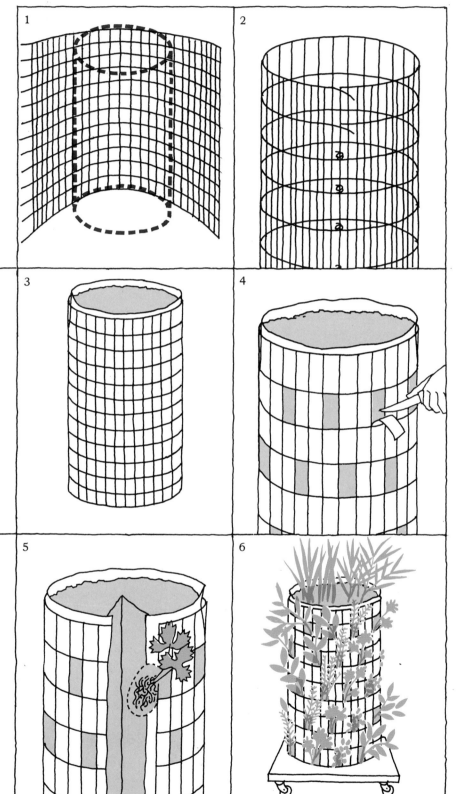

discoloration that indicates the presence of tiny red spider mites, or the wispy clouds of white flies, which may flutter away like animated snowflakes when you shake the plant. Whether you buy a plant or move one in from the garden, put it in quarantine for a couple of weeks, away from other plants, and recheck to make sure it is not bringing in any insects that might set off an epidemic among your other house plants.

If you do find that insects have taken up residence, turn the plant upside down, holding it in its pot, and swish its leaves around in a bucket of tepid soapy water (use mild soap, not a detergent). If necessary, add a pesticide such as malathion or diazinon to the water. Follow label instructions and wear rubber gloves. Scale insects, sometimes visible on the stems and backs of the leaves of such plants as sweet bay, can be scrubbed off with an old toothbrush after they have been killed by the insecticide. If the infestation persists, spray the plant outdoors; it can be brought indoors after its leaves have dried. In this way the chemicals used to control the pests will not harm human beings or pets. If this treatment fails, it is best to discard the plant.

To hold your indoor herbs, a myriad of tubs, boxes and hanging baskets are available, but the oldest and in many ways still the most versatile container is the familiar flowerpot. Old-fashioned clay pots do very well; excess water evaporates readily through their porous walls, their weight makes them harder to tip over accidentally, and their color will blend into almost any decorating scheme. In time the moisture coming through the sides may leave a deposit of whitish fertilizer salts or encourage the growth of splotches of green algae; encrusted pots can be scrubbed clean with soapy water. Soak dry clay pots in water for several hours before using; otherwise they may absorb soil moisture, robbing the plants.

Where weight is a consideration, as in small hanging gardens of herbs *(page 56)*, or a large container for a bay or orange tree that you want to move around, plastic pots are particularly useful. Their lack of porosity can also be a convenience for many herbs: since they do not transpire moisture through their sides, their contents need to be watered only one third as often as plants in clay pots. But they also increase the danger of drowning a plant by waterlogging its roots—a fate to which many herbs, with their need for good drainage, are very susceptible. Plastic pots are generally safe for herbs that can tolerate dampness, such as mints and sweet woodruff. And if you use a light, sandy soil mixture and avoid overwatering, they can be used for others as well.

CHOOSING A CONTAINER

The perfumed geraniums

Unlike the ubiquitous window-box geranium, loved for its profusion of blooms, the scented geranium is prized for its aromatic, unusually shaped foliage (although a few, like Clorinda and Mrs. Kingsley, overleaf, bear striking flowers). Some smell of roses; others, such as Snowflake *(right)* or Dr. Livingstone *(below)*, smell of rose mixed with mint or lemon. Geraniums that smell of limes, strawberries and oranges are other entries in this garden of 200 or so olfactory delights. The leaves may be narrow and fernlike *(denticulatum, right)* or broad as saucers *(tomentosum, right)*, in shades of green or speckled or rimmed with other colors. To compound their complexity, scented geraniums are actually *Pelargoniums,* a subgroup of the geranium family.

PELARGONIUM 'PRINCE RUPERT VARIEGATED'
Lemon-scented, bushy, with leaves edged in white

P. JATROPHAEFOLIUM
Shiny, deeply cut leaves, woody scent

P. RADENS 'DR. LIVINGSTONE'
Fernlike leaves, lemony rose-scent

P. TOMENTOSUM
Headiest of the peppermint scents

P. CAPITATUM 'SNOWFLAKE'
White-speckled leaves, mint-rose scent

P. DENTICULATUM FILICIFOLIUM
Fernlike leaves, intense pine aroma

P. GRAVEOLENS 'VARIEGATUM'
White-edged leaves, mint-rose aroma

P. CRISPUM VARIEGATUM
"Gooseberry" geranium, lemon scent

P. FRAGRANS 'SNOWY NUTMEG'
White-banded leaves, nutmeg aroma

P. 'CLORINDA'
Large vividly colored flowers, eucalyptus scent

P. 'SCHOTTESHAM'S PET'
Lacy translucent leaves, filbert scent

P. 'MRS. KINGSLEY'
Brilliant blossoms, delicate mint fragrance

P. 'STAGHORN OAK LEAF'
Rough-textured leaves, woodsy scent

P. BLANDFORDIANUM
Musk-scented, grayish fernlike foliage

P. GRAVEOLENS
Original rose-scented geranium

P. DENTICULATUM TOMENTOSUM
Velvety leaves, peppermint fragrance

P. VITIFOLIUM 'GRAPELEAF'
Rough-textured leaves, balsam scent

P. NERVOSUM
Lime-scented, striking flowers

P. SCARBOROVIAE
Strawberry scent, glossy crinkly leaves

63

No matter what material it is made of, any pot should have a drainage hole or holes in the bottom to prevent water from collecting inside, and a saucer or tray underneath to collect the runoff, preferably with a layer of pebbles to keep the drainage hole above the water. The riskiest containers are the glazed urns that have no drainage holes at all. To prevent water build-up, you can set a second, slightly smaller pot containing the plant inside such an urn, propping it up on a brick or a layer of pebbles.

Indoor-grown herbs require a carefully selected growing mixture. Ordinary garden soil may harbor insect eggs and weed seeds; furthermore it is generally too heavy with clay to provide sufficient drainage around the confined roots of a potted herb. Garden soil can be pasteurized in a kitchen oven, then mixed with additives to lighten it, but most indoor gardeners buy packaged potting soil, which is already pasteurized and mixed with lightening agents and nutrients. Potting soils sold for house plants generally can be used as is. If good drainage is especially urgent, as with aloe or house-leek, lighten the mixture with one part sand or perlite to three parts potting soil. For a tropical plant like jasmine, use a mix with a high organic content like that sold for African violets.

ENSURING DRAINAGE

To ensure proper drainage and prevent clogging, place a shard from an old broken clay pot, convex side up, over the hole or holes or put a ½-inch layer of small pebbles in the bottom of a small or medium-size pot; if the pot is 6 inches or more in diameter use a layer up to 1 inch deep. Add enough potting mix so that the plant will sit with the top of its soil ball ½ inch below the top of the pot; in large pots (8 inches or more) it should be 1 inch below.

If you are removing a plant from its temporary nursery container—or repotting one that has outgrown its pot—water it thoroughly a half hour ahead of time so that it will slip out of the pot easily with the soil ball clinging around its roots. If the roots are visible and crowded, growing around and around the soil ball like spaghetti, move the plant to a larger pot, or hose the roots off to remove outside dirt, then shave off the matted outer roots with a sharp knife. Trim an equal amount off the bottom; then, to keep the plant in balance, trim a roughly proportionate amount of top growth.

Set the plant in the pot you have prepared and hold it upright as you fill in with soil mix around the sides, poking it down with fingers or a stick to make sure no air pockets remain. When you have filled the pot even with the top of the soil ball, press down with both thumbs around the edge to firm the soil mix into place, then water the plant until water seeps out the drainage hole.

Once you have potted your herbs properly, you are ready to move them to the indoor locations where they will grow best. For most, that means a place where they will get as much sun as possible, and in the Northern Hemisphere that usually means centered on a south-facing window sill. The next best choice is an east- or west-facing window, though hot afternoon sun pouring in the latter for several hours a day may require that you keep watch for wilting and either move sensitive plants away from the glass or hang a sheer curtain to filter the rays. A few shade-tolerant species like mint and sweet woodruff will do reasonably well in a north window with bright light unobstructed by nearby houses or trees.

If you lack windows with the proper exposure, you can still grow herbs indoors—under artificial light. Many gardeners prefer this method because it gives them a more reliable source than natural light and results in a healthy, bushy symmetry that window sill plants sometimes do not have. To provide the full spectrum of light wavelengths that plants require, use either the special fluorescent tubes made for this purpose, or combine two ordinary tubes, one labeled "cool white" and the other "warm white." If necessary, set the potted plants on bricks or inverted pots so the tubes are an

REPOTTING TO CONTROL GROWTH

Because the roots of many herbs grow rapidly into tangled masses, frequent pruning and repotting are necessary. Knock the plant out of the pot and, with a sharp knife, cut off about one third of the root ball. Then trim the same amount of top growth.

Select a pot one inch larger in diameter. Add an inch of pebbles and a shard over the drainage hole to ensure good drainage. Then cover with enough commercial potting soil so that the top of the root ball is about an inch below the pot's rim.

Fill in more soil around the root ball, using a thick dowel to tamp the soil firmly and eliminate air pockets. Add more soil as necessary. Water the plant thoroughly, then set it in the shade for a few days until after it has become acclimatized.

USING ARTIFICIAL LIGHT

Create a kitchen herb garden by mounting a two-tube fluorescent fixture under a kitchen cabinet. Insert one "cool" and one "warm" white 20-watt, 24-inch tube. To provide humidity, place a 1-inch layer of pebbles in a waterproof tray. Place potted plants on the tray, decreasing their distance from the light source to suit their size by setting them on bricks, inverted flower pots or pieces of wood; the top leaves should be 4 to 6 inches from the tubes. Keep the lights on for 14 to 16 hours a day.

optimum 4 to 6 inches above the topmost leaves of the plants. Keep the lights on for 14 to 16 hours a day if they are the sole light source, or use them a few hours each day to supplement natural light. The fluorescent tubes should be replaced after about a year, or when they reach 70 to 80 per cent of their stated service life (usually listed in hours on the tube package); at this point they are providing 20 to 30 per cent less light than when they were new.

As important as sufficient light for herbs are proper temperature, which should be fairly low, especially at night, and humidity, which should be relatively high. Most homes are far too hot and dry in winter for plants, even those herbs that come from hot, dry Mediterranean climes. During the day the situation is rarely critical; many herbs will tolerate temperatures that go to 70° and higher. But they have evolved to require a rest in the coolness of the outdoor night, when the usual temperature during the growing season is 60° or less. The best way to ensure this is to turn the thermostat down to 60° or even 55° at night. During fuel shortages, many people who lowered their thermostats as a conservation measure discovered that their house plants flourished as never before. If you must keep your thermostat at 68° or higher night and day, keep the plants in an enclosed, unheated (but not freezing) sun porch or in a spare room where the temperature is kept lower.

Indoor atmosphere may stagnate in winter, so give the plants some fresh air by opening a window for a half hour or so once a day. But make sure they are not exposed to a direct blast of icy air; choose a window well away from the plants and open it at the top.

Many windows that are best for maximum natural light are the worst for heat, since they are located directly above radiators or warm-air vents. The heat can make the air around such a window even drier than that in the rest of the house. The way to solve both problems is to deflect the heat away from the pots and simultaneously humidify the air around the leaves. Group the pots in trays that will partially shield them from hot air and also serve as simple humidifiers. Raise the pots by covering the trays with an inch of pebbles. Keep the water level just below the bottoms of the pots, so the soil cannot draw up moisture to waterlog the roots. The evaporating moisture will help keep the relative humidity around the leaves at a beneficial 40 to 60 per cent.

WATERING REQUIREMENTS While herbs benefit from humidity around their leaves, special care must be taken that they do not get too much around their roots, whether they are set in humidity trays or not. Overwatering is the principal threat to herbs indoors, just as its concomitant, poor drainage, is the major villain outdoors. The easiest way to tell if a plant really needs water is to stick your finger a half inch into the soil; if it is dry and crumbly at that point, get out the watering can.

The best time to water is in the morning, so plants can use the moisture and nutrients in the soil during the daylight hours and so any excess moisture can evaporate readily. Water applied in the afternoon or evening tends to stand around the roots and stems overnight, inviting fungus and rot. In a warm room, plants sometimes cannot take up cold water as rapidly as they lose moisture through their leaves, so they may wilt even if the soil feels moist. To prevent this and to aid the general health of your plants, always use tepid water. To water, fill the space at the top of the pot with water up to the rim, and repeat if necessary until water begins to seep out through the bottom drainage hole; check later to make sure the plants are not standing in excess water.

If a plant has gone longer than usual between waterings, and dusty soil or wilting leaves indicate that it is bone dry, submerge the whole pot in a sink or pail of tepid water. Soak it until the air bubbles stop rising from the soil surface, then set it aside to drain for 20 minutes or half an hour. Many indoor herb gardeners give their plants such an immersion every two or three weeks, and use the opportunity to wash dust from the leaves.

FERTILIZER REQUIREMENTS

With the proper soil mix, indoor conditions and watering, your herbs will need only a little fertilizer at well-spaced intervals to supply their needs, especially if they receive less than optimum light. Most 5-10-5 or 10-20-10 fertilizers designed for house plants will do. Use the house-plant fertilizer mixed at half strength. Wait two or three weeks before feeding a newly potted plant, to give it time to reestablish its root system so that it can take up the nourishment, and do not feed any plant without watering it first, lest the concentrated chemicals burn the tender roots. Most herbs benefit from a light feeding in the fall, after they have adjusted to conditions indoors. From late autumn through early winter they will not get enough sunlight to warrant any feeding, but they can be fertilized again beginning in late winter or early spring. From spring to fall, feed about half as often as the package suggests.

By the time warm weather arrives in spring, your herbs will be ready to spend an increasing amount of time outdoors. Set them on the sill of an open window or on a terrace, bringing them in on nights when temperatures threaten to drop below 40°. If a plant has become weak and spindly and does not respond to this treatment, take a cutting to start a new plant and throw the old one away.

Making the most of the harvest 4

Herb gardening brings extra dividends. Beyond the pleasures of planting them and watching them grow are the delights of the harvest. Most herbs can be picked and used fresh or preserved in various forms for later enjoyment. In either form their uses are nearly endless, ranging from decorative scented mixtures to drink flavorings, tasty herb vinegars, butters and salts. Some people grow herbs to dry for winter bouquets. Others add them to their palette of natural vegetable dyes. Still others—since old beliefs die slowly—attribute strange powers to these ancient plants. One gardener who grows several hundred kinds of herbs at her farm in Connecticut recalls an occasion when she was asked for assistance by a distraught man who said he had lost his best friend.

"Is he dead?" the herb gardener asked.

"No, but he is so angry he won't speak to me," was the answer. He wanted an herb that would solve his problem.

Sifting through her memory of ancient lore, the herb gardener (who prefers to remain anonymous because she does not believe in such occult remedies), suggested slipping the angry one something with cumin seed in it, perhaps a tempting piece of homemade cake. The next time she saw the man, she anxiously asked him what had happened.

"Oh, it worked like a charm," the man replied. "You certainly know your herbs!"

Although the average gardener is more likely to use herbs in cooking than in witchcraft, he would be well advised to follow certain traditional practices. These culinary techniques depend, first of all, not only on the plant involved but on whether its leaves are to be used fresh or are to be preserved. For immediate use, pick leaves at any time before the plants bloom—the sooner the better in the case of those, like borage, burnet, nasturtium and dill, that are to be eaten as tender salad greens.

In a tabletop potpourri, whole roses, a rosebud (lower left) and a eucalyptus seed pod (center left) rest among the petals and leaves of roses, violas, eucalyptus, bay, artemisia and scented geraniums.

Use a sharp pair of scissors, a knife or, on softer stems, your fingernails, to snip off a sprig or two from the tops of the plants, just above a set of leaves a few inches lower down on the stalk. This process, which gardeners call pinching back, will not only provide you with tender young leaves as you need them; it will improve the plant's health and appearance by stimulating it to put out additional fresh, bushy growth. Watch also for flower buds forming on annuals like basil or on tender perennials like oregano; if you pinch them off before they bloom, the plants will reward you by continuing to produce edible leaves instead of flowering and becoming tough as seeds are set. To perpetuate annuals without having to buy a new supply of seed each year, let one or two of each kind of plant flower and go to seed naturally. You can collect the seeds and save them for later planting, but most annual herbs reseed themselves—if you let their seeds fall naturally to the ground, they will yield new plants the following spring.

HARVESTING FROM CLUMPS

Because of a special way of growing, certain herbs require a somewhat different harvesting technique. Among these are plants like chives, lovage and parsley, which send up clumps of leaves or grasslike spears directly from their roots. Do not snip off the tops, giving the plant a "haircut," for repeated harvesting in this way will shear it progressively closer to the ground. This not only reduces the leaves to unsightly, yellow-tipped stubble but also prevents them from manufacturing the food supply to be stored in the roots over the winter so the plants will have enough energy to sprout vigorously the following spring. Instead, cut whole spears from the outside of the clump, snipping them off just above ground level. This method will provide seasoning for eggs, cold soups or salads without affecting the looks or well-being of the plants.

PICKING LEAVES TO KEEP

While the leaves of most culinary herbs can be snipped at any time if they are to be used fresh, those meant to be preserved for future use, either by drying or freezing, should be harvested at special periods of growth. A few—parsley, lovage, winter savory and salad burnet, should be cut early while leaves are still tender. But most leaves are best collected for preservation just as the plants come into bloom. It is immediately before flowering that most plants contain the maximum amount of fragrant oils in their thousands of tiny leaf glands, and since some of the oil is bound to be lost in the preserving process it is well to start with leaves that are at their best.

The ideal time of day to harvest any herb for preservation is

CUTTING CHIVES AND PARSLEY

When you pick small amounts of grassy herbs such as chives, or those that send up stalks directly from the ground, such as parsley and lovage, use a special harvesting technique. Do not shear off the tops of the stalks, for the plants will then look unattractively stubby; instead, cut off individual stalks from the outside edges of the plants, just above ground level. This method not only preserves the shapes of the plants but encourages the growth of new stalks. Thus harvested, the stalks are tender right down to the ground. Indeed, parsley stalks are often substituted for parsley leaves when a deep green color would spoil the appearance of, say, a cream sauce.

early on a sunny morning, just after the dew has evaporated. Later in the day the sun's heat may release some of the oils.

When cutting for preservation, it is important not only to select the right harvesting time but also to use an appropriate picking method. Cut off annuals far enough above the ground so that some leafy growth remains; in the case of early-blooming species like chervil and summer savory, this method will leave enough of the plant to produce new growth for a second harvest later. With shrubby tender perennials like rosemary and sweet marjoram, trim a few inches off the tip of each branch as the herbs are needed. Trimming the plants in this way will encourage new growth while providing fresh leaves for the cooking pot.

Keep the cut stems of different herbs in separate bunches, and wrap them loosely in newspaper or paper bags. Bring the bunches in out of the sun as soon as possible, rinse off dirt, then spread each bunch on a table and remove any dead leaves. It is a good idea to label each batch so that you can keep track of it throughout the preserving process; as the leaves dry they will become far less recognizable and it is easy to get them mixed up.

The problem of keeping varieties separate was solved in a different way in the 19th Century by the Shakers, in the religious communes that were engaged in the commercial production of herbs during the Civil War years. A member of one of these celibate groups, Marcia Bullard, described in these words the efficient means by which the Shakers harvested their herbs: "There were herbs of many kinds. Lobelia, pennyroyal, spearmint, peppermint, catnip, wintergreen, thoroughwort, sarsaparilla and dandelion grew wild in the surrounding fields. When it was time to gather them an elderly brother would take a great wagonload of children, armed with tow sheets, to the pastures. Here they would pick the appointed herb—each one had its own day, that there might be no danger of mixing—and, when their sheets were full, drive solemnly back home again."

HANGING BUNCHES TO DRY   In those days, as now, most leaf herbs were preserved simply by letting them dry out thoroughly and then storing them in airtight containers. An easy method for plants that have long stems and dry quickly—such as savory, sage, mint, oregano and rosemary—is to arrange the cut ends in small bunches, fasten them together, then hang each bunch upside down, indoors in a dry, well-ventilated place. To support the bunches, string a length of cord or suspend a rod horizontally from the ceiling, and spread a cloth or newspapers beneath the bunches to catch dried leaves that fall off. Do not hang the bunches against a wall, which would block air circulation and interfere with complete drying. To keep dust from settling on the leaves and to catch those that fall off, some herb gardeners hang each bunch inside a paper bag generously punched with ventilation holes on the sides; the bag is suspended so the herbs dry upside down.

QUICK DRYING IN AN OVEN   Leaves that dry more slowly, such as those of parsley, lovage and basil, should be plucked from their stems at the time of harvest. They can be spread on the floor of a warm, dry attic to dry. Or, to speed the process, spread them on cookie sheets and dry them for a few minutes in a low oven (150°), leaving the door ajar. Remove the leaves as soon as they are dry to the touch so that heat does not bake out the oils.

In about two weeks, somewhat longer in humid weather, the suspended quick-drying leaves should crackle to the touch. Take each bunch down carefully, spread it on a clean cloth and strip the leaves off the stems. Some herb foliage, like the needles of rosemary, becomes hard and sharp, so you may want to protect your hands with gloves.

If you have placed the bunches in paper bags, shake each bag and listen for dried leaves falling to the bottom. When the foliage is dry and crumbly, roll the bag gently between your hands to remove most of the leaves from the stems, then empty the contents and pick off the remaining leaves.

Throw away the stems. They tend to retain some moisture

and become moldy in storage. If you like, keep some of the whole leaves in a separate jar to use for herb teas; the remaining whole or partly broken leaves can be stored as they are, or they can be crumbled between your hands or rubbed through a coarse sieve. The larger the pieces of leaves, the longer they will retain their flavor, but crumbled herbs concentrate more flavor in less volume and thus can be stored in less space.

Many gardeners dry herbs in yet another way—on stacked horizontal trays that permit ample circulation of air. This method can be used for virtually any herb but is particularly suitable for short-stemmed, wiry herbs, like creeping varieties of thyme, that cannot be readily tied in bundles. It also is helpful with plants like sweet bay, from which you may want to harvest only a few large leaves, and with lemon verbena, which should be harvested after the plant is moved indoors for the winter but before the leaves drop. For drying trays use window screens with either wood or metal frames, or make special trays by joining lengths of light lumber into frames over which screening is stapled. The trays should be set out of direct sunlight in a dry place where they can remain undisturbed for several days and where air can circulate

HANGING HERBS WITH LONG STEMS

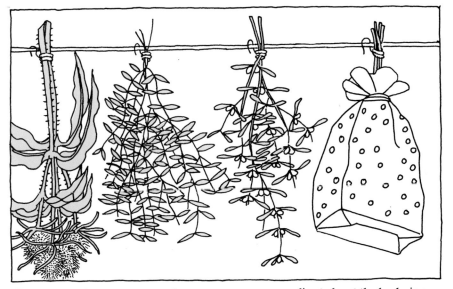

Cut herbs such as rosemary and mint just above ground level, swishing the leaves in lukewarm water. Separate each species into small bouquets held with rubber bands, which will contract as stems shrink. Use paper clips to hang the herbs in a dry, well-ventilated place such as a kitchen or attic. If seed heads might drop off, enclose the bunches in perforated paper bags (far right). The herbs will dry in a week or two.

freely over, under and through them. Prop single trays on two chairs, or for larger harvests of herbs, stack several, one on top of the other separated by blocks, or make trays that stack together on their own legs *(drawing, page 76)*.

COLLECTING SEEDS

The tray-drying method is also useful in preserving herbs grown for their flavorful seeds, among them dill, caraway, coriander, cumin and anise, as well as in collecting seeds to save for planting. When the seed heads become dry and brown or gray, and the seeds themselves have lost their greenish color and are about to drop, cut entire seed heads one at a time so they fall into a cloth-lined basket or paper bag. Some gardeners keep a supply of labeled bags on hand and gradually accumulate seed heads until they have enough to process a substantial batch. Spread the seed heads on the drying trays and keep them in a dry, well-ventilated place for five or six days. If the seeds are very small, spread cheesecloth over the screen so they do not fall through.

When the seed heads are thoroughly dry, rub them between your hands so the seeds drop onto the trays, discard the empty stems and gently shake the tray, blowing on it to winnow out the

HOW TO PICK AND DRY LEAVES

Just before the plant blooms—when its oils are heavily concentrated—cut off about one-quarter of the top of large-leaved plants; remove sprigs of small-leaved ones. As the growing season ends, cut at ground level.

Rinse off any dirt. Strip large leaves from the stem, but keep sprigs intact. Lay leaves and sprigs, one layer deep and separated so that none touch, on drying trays (page 76). Dry until the leaves are crisp.

remaining chaff. Then stack the trays again so the seeds can dry for another week or 10 days, occasionally shaking the trays so all seed surfaces are equally exposed to air.

After drying leaves or seeds, store them in tight containers that will keep them dry, free of mold and at their flavorful best. You can use decorative glass spice jars or apothecary jars, as long as the tops provide good seals, or use empty vitamin bottles or screw-top jelly jars. Larger quantities can be sealed in canning jars, flour or coffee canisters or quart-sized glass jars with screw-tops.

Glass shows off the leaves or seeds attractively and makes it easy to keep track of how much you have left. Perhaps more important, a transparent container makes it easy to check to see if moisture is condensing inside, critical during the first week or so after the herbs have been dried. If you see a mist of droplets forming inside the glass, you will know that the leaves or seeds still have some moisture in them and will soon become moldy or rot if they are left in the container; promptly pour them out and dry them for another two or three days on a drying tray, or briefly in a low oven, before returning them to storage.

COOL, SHADED STORAGE

To prolong the useful life of the dried herbs, their containers should be kept in a cool place. Glass jars should be kept out of direct sunlight, which makes the leaves fade and draws out the oils. Though such containers may be decorative with sunlight shining through them, do not put them in a kitchen window unless it is well shaded or faces north. And do not put any herb container on a shelf near a stove or other appliance that gives off heat. This is especially important for the seeds that you intend to plant; they are best stored in a cool dark place to ensure the vitality of the seed embryos while in storage.

Label each container with the name of the herb it contains and note the date when the batch was packed. Though some seeds —for example, balm, borage and coriander—keep satisfactorily for several years, leaf herbs lose most of their flavor after a year and should be discarded and replaced.

TECHNIQUES FOR FREEZING

While the leaves of most culinary herbs can be dried for later use, many can be frozen with equal ease and sometimes with better results. Many gardener-cooks prefer this method, particularly for such delicately flavored leaves as those of chives, basil, burnet, parsley, fennel and dill. Though many herbs wilt when they are frozen, and some, like basil, turn darker, their flavor will remain remarkably fresh even after a year in the freezer. Once the herbs have thawed, any leftovers should be discarded, not be refrozen.

In the days before the home freezer was a common appliance, gardeners used to preserve delicate herbs in salt—placing sprigs between layers of salt in crocks. The encrusted salt had to be washed off before the herbs could be used. Some cooks continue to use this method, but most people find it easier to store clean, fresh leaves in the freezer.

Like herbs that are to be dried, herbs to be frozen should be gathered on a sunny morning soon after the dew has disappeared; rinse off dirt, remove dead leaves and pat the sprigs dry on a paper towel. Some people maintain that the flavor is best preserved by blanching the leaves in boiling water for a minute and then plung-

MAKING DRYING TRAYS

1. *Construct simple stacking trays for curing herbs from lengths of 2-by-2 lumber and insect screening. Size is optional, but for convenient handling the trays should be no smaller than 14 by 22 inches and no larger than 24 by 36 inches. Cut framing sections and assemble them with nails or screws. Sand rough edges.*

2. *Cut the screening to measure about an inch larger than the inside frame opening. Stretch the material across the frame, then attach it with staples or carpet tacks.*

3. *Cut two more pieces of wood for the spacers, the same length as the short ends of the frame. To make the trays easier to handle, set the spacers ½ inch in from the short ends of the frame; screw them in place.*

4. *When using the trays, save space by stacking the trays one on top of the other. The spacer pieces will leave 3 inches between the levels of screening to allow air to circulate freely above and below them. (How the herbs should be arranged on each tray for proper drying is shown on page 74.)*

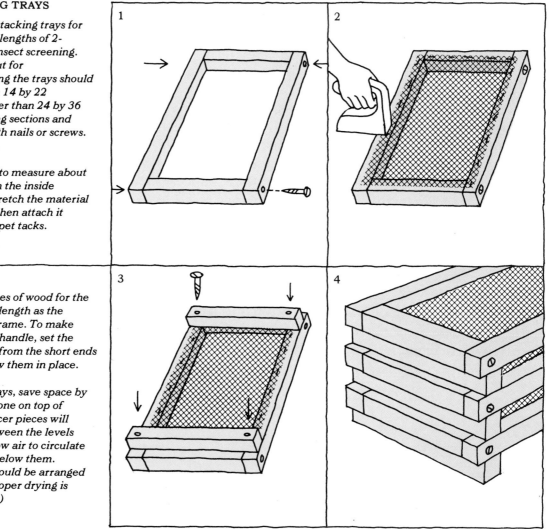

ing them into cold water. But other gardeners believe that herbs will last as long and taste even fresher if they are simply wrapped and frozen. Put small, convenient amounts in individual clear plastic sandwich bags and clip a handful of bags together or put them in a larger freezer container, adding a label with the name of the herb and the date of freezing. This way you can remove individual bags with enough leaves for one dish without having to disturb the rest of your supply.

PACKAGING MIXTURES

You can also store separate servings of herb mixtures—parsley, chives and tarragon, for example—in small packets so you do not have to find and open several different bags each time you make a dish that calls for that combination. Put the leaves or sprigs into their packages whole; they will retain their flavor a little longer that way and will be easy to chop while they are still frozen.

Fresh, dried or frozen, the culinary herbs can be used in an almost unlimited number of ways, as the recipes in any of today's cookbooks will attest. Not all cookbooks, however, provide general guidelines for using herbs. Expert cooks say that herbs should be used sparingly, to bring out and enhance the natural flavor of a dish, perhaps to give it an unexpected touch, but rarely to dominate it. It is better to err on the side of caution when it comes to using pungent herbs like rosemary, oregano, garlic and sage; a little goes a long way, and too much can make people dislike an herb or the dish it is used in.

Such overexposure to a distinctive flavor can have long-range effects. It is the reason Marie Therese Colonna, who teaches French cooking in Falls Church, Virginia, does not include in her course a dish that is a classic of French cuisine: chicken with tarragon. Mme. Colonna explains that tarragon, which has a flavor somewhat like licorice or anise, reminds her of a visit she had with her cousin in Paris when she was 16 years old. "He offered me a glass of Pernod, which is flavored with anise," she said. "Instead of one glass, I drank four. From that day to this I have not been able to eat, drink or smell anise or licorice or tarragon without remembering the terrible illness of that afternoon."

EXTRA FLAVOR FROM DRYING

When experimenting with a new recipe, use a little less than the instructions call for; it is easy enough to add more of an herb to taste. Be especially careful when using dried herbs, which, despite the loss of some of their oils, are usually stronger than fresh ones if the same volume measures are compared. Their oils become concentrated as the leaves shrivel and crumble, losing moisture. As a general rule, ¼ teaspoon of a dried, finely powdered herb is roughly equivalent to ¾ to 1 teaspoon of dried and loosely crumbled leaves, and to 1½ to 2 teaspoons of fresh chopped leaves. Frozen leaves may lose a little flavor, but they can be used in the amounts specified for fresh leaves. If you are trying out a recipe that is vague as to amounts, or if you are creating a recipe of your own, a safe rule of thumb is to use no more than ¼ teaspoon of a dried herb, or 1 teaspoon of a chopped fresh or frozen herb, to every four servings.

Every cook develops personal ideas about which herbs to use in which dishes, but certain herbs have proved to be good companions for certain foods—chives with eggs, basil with tomatoes, tarragon with chicken, mint with cucumbers, and so on. As you become more familiar with the distinctive tastes of specific herbs, you may want to experiment with some variations of your own, but it is best to remember that extremely pungent herbs such as rosemary, sage and thyme are rarely used together because their competing flavors tend to clash.

Some herb mixtures, of course, are basics of good French cooking—for example, *fines herbes* and *bouquet garni*. The former

HOW TO SEPARATE THE SEEDS

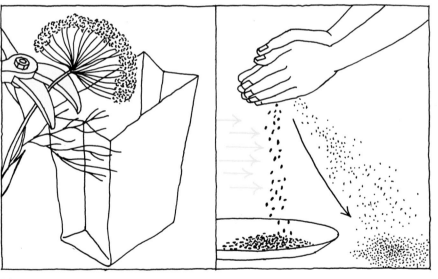

Pick the seeds of herbs such as dill, coriander, anise and caraway when capsules begin to open. Cut the stems an inch or two below the seed heads, bending the stalks so seeds drop into a paper bag.

Hang the bag in a dry place for a week. Then set a large bowl in a light breeze and rub the heads between your hands; the breeze will blow the chaff aside while seeds fall into the bowl. Dry seeds and seal in jars.

are blends of compatible flavors, often used in egg and cheese dishes or sprinkled over casseroles or fish. Each blend usually includes one member of the allium family, such as chives, one member of the parsley family, such as curly- or flat-leaved parsley or chervil, and one, two or even three others with distinctive flavors, such as tarragon, basil, sweet marjoram, thyme, savory or burnet. A classic mixture, called ravigote and used for meat, poultry, fish and vegetables, is generally a blend of chives, chervil, tarragon and burnet. Another blend, especially good with stews and soups, is half lovage and half parsley. Blends of *fines herbes* can be made of chopped fresh or frozen leaves, or of dried leaves; to release their flavor at the right moment they are usually sprinkled into a dish during the last few minutes of cooking, or over an omelette just before it is folded and served.

A *bouquet garni* is a mixture of several herbs—fresh, frozen or dried—that is added to soups, stews and other dishes while they are cooking but is removed before the dish is served. A basic bouquet can be made by tying together three or four sprigs of parsley or chervil, a couple of sprigs of thyme (or several blades of chives for a delicate onion flavor), and one sweet-bay leaf. Use light cotton string or heavy thread and leave several inches attached so you can pull the bouquet out of the pot when the flavoring has been done. This combination is often varied or added to; a sprig of basil for tomatoes, one of marjoram or tarragon for poultry, one of rosemary for lamb or beef.

A BOUQUET FOR STEWS

For a basic bouquet of dried herbs, mix ½ cup of dried parsley or chervil with ¼ cup of thyme leaves and half a bay leaf. Place this blend on a double thickness of cheesecloth 3 inches square, gather up the sides and tie it with string or heavy thread to make a little bag, leaving a few inches of loose string for pulling the bag out of the pot.

Alone or in combinations, herbs can be used not only to season various cooked dishes but to add their flavors to vinegars, dressings, spreads and drinks.

Herb vinegars can be made from virtually any culinary herb. Mint vinegar is good with lamb, ham or cole slaw; a dash of basil vinegar gives a glass of tomato juice or a tomato aspic an added tang; garlic vinegar with oil and a little pepper and salt makes a tasty French dressing. Some herbs add color as well as special flavor: purple basil makes clear vinegar a rich ruby red and chive blossoms turn the liquid a delicate pink.

PREPARING HERB VINEGARS

The simplest way to make herb vinegar is to place several sprigs of leaves (or a couple of garlic or shallot cloves) in a bottle with a non-metal top, fill it with white distilled vinegar and set it aside in a cool dark place for several weeks. If you use cider or wine vinegar, add herbs with stronger flavors, such as mint, bay or basil. To speed the process, crush the leaves or cloves, and heat the vinegar to just below the boiling point before adding the herbs and bottling. Strain out the crushed residue after about 10 days and rebottle. Leave a few sprigs or blossoms floating in the bottles for decoration.

Herbed butter—ordinary butter flavored with different herbs or combinations like *fines herbes*—adds a marvelous flavor to hot French bread, and it is delicious when melted over broiled hamburgers. Simply add minced herbs to butter that has been allowed to warm to room temperature. For each ¼-pound stick, use 4 tablespoons of fresh leaves or 2 tablespoons of dried leaves, though a tablespoon of strong fresh herbs like oregano, thyme or garlic will suffice. Add a little lemon juice and beat in a bowl or whirl in an electric blender until fluffy and smooth, then place in a covered container in the refrigerator.

Chopped fresh herbs like chives, parsley, basil and dill can also be mixed into cream cheese for salads or for hors d'oeuvre spreads, as well as into mayonnaise, Russian dressing, hollandaise or mustard sauce and marinades. A favorite of many cooks is the sauce called *pesto* or *pistou,* based on basil, garlic, cheese and olive

(continued on page 86)

Herbs preserved

The ultimate fate of most herbs is to end as a memory. They become unseen ingredients in savory stews or whiffs of fragrance from a sachet hidden in a bureau drawer. But occasionally an herb product capitalizes on the charm of the living plant. Herbalist Adelma Simmons flavors jellies with infusions of herbs, then tucks a sprig of the actual plant into the top of each jar as a sort of label (right). Her glittering condiments, made on a simple apple-juice base, include a golden woodruff jelly to serve with game, another golden jelly of tarragon for fish or chicken, a ruby-red rosemary jelly to accompany turkey, and a green basil jelly to glorify hamburger. Other herbal products that perpetuate the plant material of which they are made include a splendid jug of vinegar flavored and decorated with several herbs (overleaf), and on pages 84–85, three arrangements made from dried herbs—a "tussie mussie" for a bride to carry, a braided wreath to grace a holiday table, and a composition of pressed herb flowers and foliage pretty enough to frame.

Brilliant as stained glass in the sun, a pyramid of herbal jellies decorates an herb-framed window.

A flavoring that labels itself

Vinegar, a classic preservative for foods of every kind, here preserves the very plants that give the condiment a unique flavor. Trapped in the jug at right are sprays of dill, basil and salad burnet, a combination that adds finesse to a bowl of salad greens. Choosing herbs for such compounded vinegars is partly a matter of blending compatible flavors and partly a matter of selecting plants that complement each other visually. No less fascinating to look at and use but simpler to assemble are vinegars flavored with single herbs. A spray of mint or sage, or a cluster of chive leaves, makes a vinegar to tempt the talents of a chef and to put proudly on kitchen display.

Salad burnet contributes cucumber flavor.

Dill, synonymous with pickles, adds pungency and decorative punch.

Crinkly-leaved basil, redolent of summer, tastes warm and sweet.

The dill, salad burnet and basil aswirl in the jug at right were picked at their prime, washed to remove dust and insects, then dried thoroughly. The vinegar is store-bought white-wine vinegar, chosen for its clarity, but white-malt vinegar could be used instead. To assemble the components, first tuck the herbs into the jug, then pour in the liquid, shaking lightly to remove air bubbles from the plants. Steeping time varies with the intensity of the herb from a few weeks to several months.

Unexpected delights for the eye

The beribboned nosegay of herbs below was designed for a bride to carry at her wedding—an accessory not quite as unconventional as it seems. It includes rosemary, an herb standing for devotion and fidelity that traditionally trimmed the banquet halls at medieval marriages, and myrtle, which has been worn by brides in many cultures for centuries. Such an unexpected bouquet is only one example of the beauty that the artist's eye can find in these mundane plants. Other decorative uses for herbs include the autumnal wreath of dried herbs encircling the candle at right, and at the lower right, pressed under glass, an artful display of common herbs, many of them culinary.

Lance-shaped rosemary leaves denote fidelity.

A bouquet for a bride mingles the aromatic foliage—and traditional associations—of sage, thyme, rosemary and myrtle with tiny crepe-paper-like flowers of pearly everlasting and dainty rosebuds. In England, such herbal nosegays are often called tussie mussies, a name whose origins are an etymological mystery.

Artemisia bears flower spikes.

Clusters top garlic chives.

Braided together while their stems are still supple, the dried herbs in this wreath include rusty-red oregano, woolly white lamb's ears and the brown seed heads of Achillea filipendula. The flower spikes in the foreground are artemisia, the clusters of pale brown flowers are garlic chives, the white flower clusters are sneezewort and the prickly pods are teasel.

Reading clockwise from the sprays of dill at top right, the herbs in this dried arrangement include fan-shaped lady's mantle foliage lying on gray santolina; the spear-shaped compound leaves of vitex; and lamb's ears lying atop a sprig of thyme. Above the lamb's ears in ascending order are sage, salad burnet and rue. The spiky blossoms scattered throughout are heather.

A tint of purple colors sage.

Lamb's ears are woolly.

PESTO FOR PASTA

The classic Genovese sauce known as pesto is made with fresh basil leaves, although marjoram or dill is sometimes substituted. Customarily spooned over pasta, this pungent green sauce is also used, a dollop at a time, to flavor soup or eggplant.

To make 1½ to 2 cups of sauce combine:

2 cups fresh basil leaves stripped from their stems, coarsely chopped and tightly packed
1 teaspoon salt
½ teaspoon freshly ground black pepper
1 to 2 teaspoons finely chopped garlic
2 tablespoons freshly chopped pine nuts
1 to 1½ cups olive oil
½ cup freshly grated imported sardo, romano or Parmesan cheese

If making the pesto sauce in a blender, combine all the ingredients in the blender jar and blend at high speed until reduced to a thick sauce. To make by hand, crush the basil leaves into a smooth paste in a mortar and pestle; gradually work in the remaining ingredients.

When your supply of fresh basil leaves runs low, try stretching it with an equal amount of fresh Italian parsley for a basil-parsley pesto. And for a taste of summer in midwinter, freeze pesto in small jars.

oil. A classic North Italian recipe for this sauce is given at left.

Herb jellies and jams are old favorites. To add the flavor of such fresh leaves as thyme or rosemary, follow a standard recipe for the preserve, but just before the liquid comes to a full boil, add a cupful of leaves and then continue cooking as directed in the recipe. Finally, strain the herb-preserve mixture through several layers of damp cheesecloth before pouring it into jelly glasses and sealing with paraffin. To flavor with mint, basil or parsley, brew a tea first (see directions below), then strain it and use the liquid in place of the water called for in the standard recipe.

For a decorative touch, place a leaf of sage or scented geranium or a sprig of sweet woodruff in the bottom of each jelly glass, and pour the hot preserve over it; the leaves not only will add their own taste and scent but will serve as identifying accents visible through the clear jelly. A number of herbs can be used with apple jelly; other combinations include thyme with grape or elderberry jelly, marjoram with lemon or grapefruit, and rosemary with orange or lemon preserves.

Almost any of the sweet-scented herbs—rose geranium, rose petals, mint or lemon verbena—impart a delicate flavor to granulated sugar used to sweeten desserts and drinks, or to confectioners' sugar used in cookies, icings and cakes. Put a few leaves or petals in a screw-top jar along with the sugar and it will soon take on a pleasant hint of their fragrance.

For a different kind of last-minute seasoning to sprinkle on stews, casseroles and other dishes or to use at the table, mix several finely ground dried herbs like parsley, basil and oregano— about a tablespoon of each, along with a little pepper or paprika— with a cup of ordinary salt; store in a shaker.

The fresh leaves of many herbs have long been used to flavor ordinary tea, hot or iced, or to make distinctive teas of their own. Among those often used to make hot herbal teas, called tisanes, are sage, anise, mint, catnip, savory, marjoram, rosemary, thyme and bee balm. The last was brewed to make an American Indian beverage, known as Oswego tea and was drunk by 18th Century colonists to protest British taxes on Oriental tea.

Herb teas are made the same way as ordinary tea. But more leaves are required—about 2 teaspoons of freshly cut or frozen leaves or 1 teaspoon of dried leaves per 6-ounce serving. When herb teas are made with seeds or roots instead of leaves, it is necessary to make a decoction rather than an infusion—that is, the herb is added to water in a pot and boiled for 15 or 20 minutes to draw out the flavor of the fragrant oils.

Some connoisseurs of herb tea find it stimulating, while others say that it is relaxing. But all agree it is a conversation starter. Herbs are so rich in symbolism that Adelma Simmons, author and professional herb grower, sometimes serves what she calls Caprilands tea at her herb farm. It is a blend of equal parts of mint (for wisdom), rosemary (for remembrance), sage (for immortality and domestic happiness), thyme (for bravery), marjoram (for happiness), calendula (for a bright outlook and a good complexion) and chamomile (for soothed nerves and a good night's sleep).

The fragrant and decorative uses of herbs are almost as numerous as their culinary ones. Not only can attractive and sweet-smelling herbs be grown as house plants, but the leaves, flowers and even the roots of many of them can be preserved in scented potpourris, sachets and pillows.

WAYS TO PERFUME THE AIR

A few decades ago almost every living room and boudoir displayed at least one jar filled with a mixture of rose petals, herb leaves and spices ready to perfume the room whenever the top was removed. Such potpourris of mingled fragrances are easy to make, easier today than in the past.

The old-fashioned moist method, like that for preserving delicate culinary herbs, called for packing layers of partly dried leaves and petals between layers of salt in a crock; the process derived its name, from the French for pot and *pourrir*, to rot. Most people today, however, prefer the simpler method of drying the petals and leaves, which preserves the fragrances and colors just as well but with much less fuss.

POTPOURRI INGREDIENTS

Almost any sweet-scented herb—orange mint, thyme, rosemary, rose geranium, lemon verbena, lemon balm, sweet marjoram, sweet basil, tarragon—can provide dried leaves for making potpourri. But the traditional starting ingredient is rose petals. To them are added flowers of lavender, lemon verbena or rose geranium, which also hold their fragrance well when dried, or almost any other garden blossom notable for its scent or color. Snip flowers through the summer as they come into bloom, selecting only the freshest, most fragrant ones when they are at their peak; the best roses to use are old-fashioned favorites like the apothecary rose and the damask rose, less flamboyant than modern hybrids but considerably more fragrant.

Pick the blossoms on a dry morning after the dew is off the petals and before the sun is high; remove the petals and place them in thin layers on drying trays like those used for leaf herbs and seeds *(page 76)*. Stir the petals every day or two so they dry evenly; if a draft threatens to blow them off the tray, cover them lightly with a piece of cheesecloth. In four or five days they should be as dry and crackly as cornflakes. As you accumulate dried petals, keep each kind stored separately in an airtight container such as a quart mayonnaise jar, and keep the container away from light and heat.

DRYING FLOWERS AND BUDS

Since the petals of some flowers retain their fragrance but lose their color when dried, many gardeners also dry whole blossoms that will provide decorative accents in the finished jar—red bee balm, blue borage, orange calendulas, and violets, as well as flowers of nonherbs like bachelor's buttons and delphiniums. To dry whole flowers, place them face down in a box or tray on ½ inch of fine sand, borax or silica gel, then add enough additional sand, borax or gel to cover them. Keep the blossoms in a dry, warm place for a couple of weeks until they are well dried, then carefully remove them and store them in lidded containers until you are ready to use them.

HOW TO FIX THE SCENT

To make a potpourri, empty some dried leaves and petals into a large bowl and mix them thoroughly until you get a combination of fragrances and colors that you like. To blend the scents and make them last, you will have to add a fixative; those most readily available at drugstores and garden stores are ground orris root, from the root of the Florentine iris, and gum benzoin, a resin from a Southeast Asian tree. Add about 2 tablespoons of crushed root or gum to each quart of flower petals and herb leaves.

When all the ingredients are well mixed, store them in one or more large lidded jars, keeping them less than full so you can shake or stir the mixture two or three times a week. After five or six weeks the potpourri will have cured and blended sufficiently so you can pour it into a bowl once more, give it a final stirring and ladle it into decorative containers. Keep the containers covered, opening them only when you want the soft fragrance to permeate a room.

If you have a large supply of the potpourri mixture and if the ingredients are fairly bulky, you can use it to stuff small decorative pillows for a bedroom. The pillow covers should be made of a fabric porous enough to release the fragrance of the potpourri but firm enough to prevent crumbled leaves from escaping.

Smaller amounts of a potpourri mixture can be put into sachets to scent closets or dresser drawers. The mixture will repel moths if you include more pungent herbs like tansy, southernwood, wormwood, lavender, lavender cotton, rosemary and thyme or, best of all, *Artemisia camphorata,* which smells like camphor. To make a sachet, put a handful of dried leaves and petals in the center of a handkerchief-sized cloth, gather the corners and tie tightly with a ribbon, leaving a loop that can be slipped over the neck of an ordinary clothes hanger. For sachets that will lie flat in a drawer or linen chest, or under a bed pillow, stitch the material into an envelope 3 to 6 inches square, leaving one end open, then stuff the dried mixture into the opening and stitch it closed.

FRAGRANCE FOR THE BATH

Sachets for scenting a bath can be made quite simply by tying handfuls of dried leaves or petals in squares of cheesecloth; drop one of these little bags under the hot-water tap as you start to fill the tub, then swish it around before climbing in.

For a refreshing after-bath lotion, crush a handful of fresh or dried aromatic leaves and put it in a lidded jar with rubbing alcohol; let the jar stand for a week or so, shaking it occasionally, then strain the scented, delicately colored liquid into small stoppered bottles for use.

Fragrant herbs such as rosemary, thyme, comfrey, basil and mint can lend a refreshing scent and color to soap. To make a semisoft herbal soap, prepare an extract by adding 2 ounces of shredded herb leaves to 16 ounces of boiling water. Cover the pot, remove from the heat, then let the leaves steep for 30 minutes. Strain out and discard the leaves, and add enough water to the extract to make 12 ounces.

In the top of a double boiler, combine the herbal liquid with 3 ounces (by weight) of white floating bath soap cut into small pieces. Melt this mixture over boiling water until it is smooth. Then pour it into a widemouthed container and let it stand, uncovered, until it is cool.

HOLIDAY TRADITIONS

Some gardeners make their own tussie-mussies, old-fashioned bouquets of fresh herbs *(page 84),* to give to a bride. Others celebrate the holidays with fragrant pomanders or spice balls—whole oranges, apples or lemons stuck solidly with cloves and trimmed with sprigs of scented herbs—or "kissing balls" made of small-mesh chicken wire stuffed with moist sphagnum moss and planted with cuttings of rosemary, lavender cotton and mistletoe. Along with a festive wassail bowl of herb-spiced punch, a wreath of dried artemisia and a succulent roast flavored with thyme or sage, they are among the many joyous traditions that for centuries have rounded out the gardener's herbal year.

An illustrated encyclopedia of herbs 5

Whether you are looking for a particular cooking herb, an aromatic ground cover, a plant with unusual foliage or flowers, or one that will grow on the window sill as well as in the garden, the encyclopedia that follows will help you to make a choice. It describes the characteristics of 126 herbs and explains in detail how to grow and use them.

Each entry indicates whether the herb is an annual, a biennial or a perennial and describes where it will grow in the United States and Canada (climate requirements are keyed to the zone map on page 150). If the plant is suitable for indoor gardening, its light preferences are given, along with special soil or humidity needs.

Most herbs need abundant sunlight and a well-drained garden soil with a pH of about 6.0 to 7.5, neither very acid nor very alkaline. Otherwise they are undemanding. Generally they do not need to be fertilized. When fertilizer is used, it is commonly an organic supplement, such as compost or manure, which also helps to improve drainage, or a basic 5-10-5 fertilizer. For indoor plants, a standard commercial potting soil is usually recommended.

Entries also specify whether plants should be purchased from a nursery or propagated from seed, rooted stem cuttings or root divisions. The time of year for planting is generally determined by the date of the first or last frost, as shown on the maps on page 151. In addition, if the herb is one to be harvested, the entry gives the time and method, as well as the average crop of leaves or seeds.

The herbs are listed alphabetically according to their Latin botanical names and are grouped by genus. For example, tarragon and its relative wormwood are included in one entry, *Artemisia*. This genus name is followed by the species names, *A. absinthium* (wormwood) and *A. dracunculus* (tarragon). Because many herbs are more commonly known by their less precise English names, these are cross-referenced.

The harvest from an herb garden includes rosemary and basil, top left, and feathery dill, top right. Spriggy thyme and gray-green sage are at the bottom, and in the center are two fluffy flower heads of chives.

YARROW
Achillea millefolium

SWEET FLAG
Acorus calamus

ANISE HYSSOP
Agastache foeniculum

A

AARON'S ROD See *Verbascum*

ACHILLEA

A. millefolium (yarrow, milfoil)

Yarrow is a rugged perennial, cultivated today mainly for dried and fresh flower arrangements. This pungent plant grows 2 to 3 feet tall, with a profusion of fernlike gray-green leaves 2 to 3 inches long. From spring through midfall, its tiny muddy-white or pink blossoms form flat-topped umbrella-shaped clusters 2 to 3 inches in diameter.

HOW TO GROW. Yarrow thrives in Zones 3–10. It needs full sun and grows rapidly in well-drained, poor to average soil. It tolerates drought well. The plants can be started from seeds, but take a year or two to develop fully. More often they are propagated when root clumps are divided, as they should be in the spring every two to four years to prevent overcrowding. Plant the segments 1 to 2 feet apart at the same depth they were previously growing. To dry the flowers, cut them at their peak before they start to fade and hang them head-down in clusters of six to 12 in a dry, airy place out of the sun.

ACORUS

A. calamus (sweet flag, calamus)

Sweet flag is a hardy perennial swamp or bog plant whose lemon-scented leaves and fragrant (but rather bitter-tasting) root often are used for sachets, flavorings, medicines and candy. Calamus root long was used in a home remedy for colic. Clumps of erect, sword-shaped leaves are usually about 2 feet tall but can grow twice that in rich soil. The cylindrical flower spike, 2 to 4 inches long and studded with tiny greenish-yellow blossoms, angles out from the long stem. The creeping root has brownish-red bark and a white, fleshy interior. Usually 1 or 2 inches thick, it can reach a length of several feet in mature plants.

HOW TO GROW. Sweet flag can be grown from Zones 3–10. It flourishes in very muddy soil and full sun. It will grow in any rich garden soil that is kept moist but flowers only when growing in water. In the fall or early spring, set root divisions a foot apart and 4 to 6 inches deep. Clumps of sweet flag will increase in size rapidly because of the fast-spreading roots. Leaves to be used for flavoring may be picked at any time during the growing season. Roots are harvested in early spring or late fall after two or three years' growth, and are dried and pulverized for sachets.

AGASTACHE

A. foeniculum, also called *A. anethiodora* (anise hyssop, fennel hyssop)

Anise hyssop is a handsome 2½- to 3-foot-tall perennial with anise-scented foliage that can be used to brew aromatic tea or to garnish fruit cups. The coarsely toothed oval leaves, approximately 3 inches long, are green in color, with soft, white undersides. In midsummer, many flower spikes studded with tiny lavender double-lobed blossoms attract bees with their sweet-scented nectar. Each blossom has two pairs of protruding stamens, giving the plant its only resemblance to true hyssop. The botanical name refers to fennel *(Foeniculum vulgare),* which anise hyssop resembles in its scent.

HOW TO GROW. Anise hyssop can be grown in Zones 3–8. It adapts readily to any kind of soil. It does best in cool weather and a sunny location, though it tolerates light shade. Grown from seeds, the plants take two years to bloom. Sow the seeds in the fall where the plants are to remain; they will lie dormant through the winter, sprouting in the early spring.

Thin them to stand a foot apart. Alternatively, transplant nursery-grown seedlings, spacing them 1 to 2 feet apart. Until they bloom, they can be transplanted easily, as can seedlings that arise from the plant's own seeds.

AGRIMONIA
A. eupatoria (agrimony, cocklebur, church steeples)

Agrimony is a spiky, 2- to 3-foot-tall perennial with delicately apricot-scented leaves and flowers. In one old herbal it is recommended as being "good for naughty livers," but is now used as a dye yielding a yellow hue when gathered late in the growing season. Its green stalk is flanked by sets of compound leaves that graduate in size from 3 inches per set at the top to 7 or 8 inches at the bottom. The bottom sets of leaves are complex in structure, with pairs of small leaflets and pairs of saw-toothed large leaflets alternating along the leaf stem. In summer, tiny yellow blossoms form a spike along the top of the hairy stalk, a characteristic fancifully interpreted to arrive at the common name of church steeples. In time these blossoms produce hooked seed pods that inspired the name of cocklebur.

HOW TO GROW. Agrimony can be grown in Zones 3–8. It is easily cultivated in ordinary dry soil and will tolerate slight shade, but does better in full sun. Collect seeds from the dried stalk in the fall and plant them ¼ inch deep and 7 inches apart in the spring. The plant also seeds itself readily. For quicker propagation, divide the roots early in the spring and set the segments 7 to 9 inches apart.

AJUGA
A. reptans (ajuga, bugleweed, bugle)

Ajuga is a creeping perennial that covers the ground so thickly it prevents weeds from growing and makes a popular ground cover. It is also widely—but mistakenly—planted in rock gardens, where it smothers adjacent plants. The root can be used to produce a black dye for woolens. Ajuga's shiny, oval-shaped leaves, 2 to 4 inches long, form flat rosette clumps that spread outward through a network of runners. Its foliage ranges in color from a deep green through shades of reddish-purple, depending on the season of the year. In spring, brilliant blue flowers cover short spiky stems 5 to 6 inches high. Hybridized varieties of the original herb are available with purple, red or white blossoms and foliage that ranges in color from deep burgundy to green variegated with white and pink.

HOW TO GROW. Ajuga grows in Zones 3–10. It flourishes under a wide range of conditions—in full sun or heavy shade and in moist or dry soil. Set young plants bought from a nursery 6 to 12 inches apart. The new young plants that appear at the ends of runners can easily be cut free for transplanting in the spring or fall.

ALCHEMILLA
A. vulgaris (lady's mantle)

A graceful hardy perennial, 6 to 12 inches tall, this ground-hugging plant derives its common name from the fan-shaped, pleated leaves that were thought to resemble the folds of a medieval cloak. Tiny hairs give the leaves a silvery sheen and collect sparkling droplets of dew or rain that remain through the day; this liquid was prized by alchemists, hence the Latin name, *Alchemilla.* Today, the plant is valued for its large leaves, as much as 6 inches in diameter, which make a handsome ground cover. In late spring and occasionally as late as fall it bears airy clusters of small yellow blossoms, each flower only ⅛ inch in diameter. The flowers are often dried for use in winter arrangements.

AGRIMONY
Agrimonia eupatoria

AJUGA
Ajuga reptans

For climate zones and frost dates, see maps, pages 150–151.

LADY'S MANTLE
Alchemilla vulgaris

SHALLOT
Allium ascalonicum

TOP ONION
Allium cepa aggregatum

HOW TO GROW. This cold-loving plant grows wild in eastern Canada and New England; it can be cultivated successfully in Zones 3–8. It tolerates shade and will grow and spread rapidly in any well-drained soil. Start seedlings in a greenhouse or cold frame in the early spring, thinning them to stand 2 inches apart. Move them outside when the first true leaves develop, planting them 4 to 6 inches apart. Lady's mantle can also be propagated by carefully dividing root clumps in the spring, setting rooted segments 4 to 6 inches apart to produce a thick ground cover quickly. To harvest flowers for winter bouquets, cut them at the peak of their bloom and hang them upside down to dry in a dark, airy room. Individual leaves can be dried between layers of paper for decorative use.

Lady's mantle can be grown indoors in a deep pot placed in a cool location. It should be fed with a liquid plant food high in nitrogen, such as 30-10-10. Keep the soil damp in spring and summer, somewhat drier in winter.

ALECOST See *Chrysanthemum*
ALKANET See *Anchusa*
ALL-HEAL See *Valeriana*

ALLIUM

A. ascalonicum (shallot); *A. cepa aggregatum*, also called *A. cepa viviparum* (top onion, Egyptian onion); *A. porrum* (leek); *A. sativum* (garlic); *A. schoenoprasum* (chive)

These five relatives of the onion are all perennials except for leek, a biennial. Three of them—shallot, top onion and garlic—are grown for their flavorsome bulbs, though the young leaves are also used in salads. The chive plant's hollow, grasslike leaves are chopped for seasoning, and its neat clumps and decorative lavender blossoms make it desirable for borders and cut flowers. Leeks are cultivated for their cylindrical stems, 6 to 10 inches long, which are used both as vegetable and seasoning.

Shallot, the most delicately flavored of the onions, has a compound bulb divided into segments called cloves, each with its own purplish parchment-like covering. The hollow, cylindrical, blue-green leaves form clumps about 18 inches tall. Flowers are rare, but tiny purple or white blossoms sometimes appear in late spring or early summer.

Garlic, like shallot, has a compound bulb that is divided into cloves, which are enclosed in a white or mottled-purple parchment-like covering. The sparse, flat leaves grow 18 inches tall, and bear the unmistakable garlic flavor and odor when they are crushed. In the early summer, a small spherical cluster of white or pinkish flowers may appear at the top of a thin stalk.

Chives, the smallest of the onions, appear each growing season in lush, grasslike clumps 8 to 12 inches high. Its fluffy balls of flowers, ¾ to 1 inch in diameter, bloom on tall, slender stems in the late spring. A clump of chives that measures 5 inches in diameter will provide 3 to 5 cups of leaves at the first cutting.

Top onion is an odd-looking onion, forming a crown of small brown bulbils at the top of a 2- to 3-foot tubular stem called a scape. As the weight of this bulbous head increases, the entire scape dips to the ground and the bulbils take root to produce new plants. The top onion's hollow, dark blue-green leaves, swollen at the base, reach only halfway up the scape; the underground bulb develops hardly at all. The bulbils give a delicate flavor to cooked dishes or salads and are sometimes pickled as cocktail onions.

The leek, the one biennial in this group of onions, has straplike leaves 2 to 3 feet tall. If the leek remains in the ground a second season, it develops a flower stalk from which emerges a globe-shaped mass, ranging from 3 to 4 inches wide, consisting of numerous tiny purple blossoms.

HOW TO GROW. All five plants thrive in Zones 3–10, and they tolerate the hot, humid climate of the Gulf Coast. They grow best in full sun and rich soil, and should be planted in the early spring.

Shallots do well in soil with a pH of 5.5 to 7.0. Plants started from seed require two years to mature, and most shallots are consequently grown from cloves; if started from cloves planted in the fall, shallots mature in about nine months. When planted in the spring, shallots mature in three or four months but the clusters are smaller. Plant the cloves 2 to 3 inches apart at a depth of about 2 inches. When the leaves are 5 to 6 inches tall, apply 5-10-5 fertilizer at the rate of 3 ounces per 10 feet of row. By midsummer the shallots will have formed clusters of 3 to 10 cloves. When the foliage becomes partially withered, dig the cloves up and cure them by placing them in a dry, shady spot for two to three weeks before storing.

Garlic is grown in a similar way in soil with a pH of 5.5 to 8.0. Break a garlic bulb into single cloves and place each clove 1 inch deep and 4 to 6 inches apart. Fertilize, using the same procedure as shallot. When the leaves turn yellow, dig up the plant and store as for shallot. To speed ripening, bend down the tops of the plant as they begin to turn yellow to limit the plant's growth.

Chives grow best in soil with a pH of 6.0 to 7.0. Propagated from seed, they take about a year to produce harvest-ready leaves. Sow the seeds in rows in the spring, covering them with ¼ to ½ inch of soil. Do not thin the plants the first year. Early the following spring, transplant small clusters of seedlings 5 to 6 inches apart, leaving six or more bulbs in each cluster. Chives planted as rooted clumps—the more common procedure—are set about 2 inches deep, also 5 to 6 inches apart. Though chives are planted in the spring in most parts of the country, in very warm regions where the summer temperature remains over 90° for prolonged periods, they can be planted in the fall for a winter harvest. Chives spread rapidly in rich, moist soil. Should the plants weaken from repeated cutting, scratch a light dusting of 5-10-5 fertilizer into the soil. Renew the plants every two to four years by dividing the roots and resetting them into soil that has been enriched with an abundance of organic matter.

Top onion grows best in soil with a pH of 6.0 to 7.0. Set the bulbils in rows 4 to 8 inches apart and ½ inch deep, in late summer, fall or spring. During the summer, treat the same way as shallots. When new bulbils appear in late summer, cut off the entire top growth; fresh leaves will appear to permit a continuing harvest of greens. The stalks, with their clusters of bulbils, may be hung in a cool, dry place for use during the winter.

Leek does best in a moist, fertile soil with a pH of 6.0 to 8.0. For a midsummer crop, sow leek seeds indoors about two months before the last frost is expected. When the seedlings have reached a height of 4 to 5 inches, prepare a trench 12 inches deep and 6 inches wide and fill in the bottom 6 inches with a layer of compost. Set the seedlings 4 to 6 inches apart in the trench. If more than one row is required, allow 15 to 18 inches between the trenches. You can sow seeds directly outdoors when night temperatures no longer fall below freezing, or in frost-free regions when daytime temperatures average no higher than 80°, spacing them in groups of three to four seeds, 4 to 6 inches apart, and covering them with ⅛ inch of soil. When the seeds sprout, thin each group to one seedling. As the plants mature, fill the

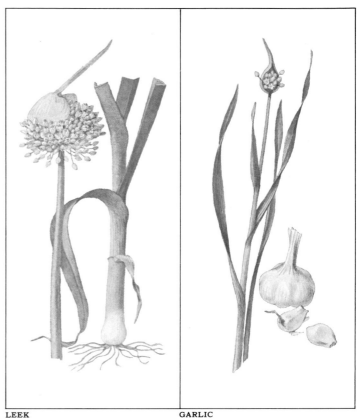

LEEK
Allium porrum

GARLIC
Allium sativum

CHIVE
Allium schoenoprasum

For climate zones and frost dates, see maps, pages 150–151.

ALOE
Aloe vera

MARSH MALLOW
Althaea officinalis

trench gradually to shield the bases of the plants from light and blanch them. Every three to four weeks scatter 5 ounces of 5-10-5 fertilizer per 10 feet of row along each side. Leeks mature in four and one-half months but are edible at any stage; when they are young, they are sometimes used as a substitute for scallions.

Chives, top onion and garlic can be grown successfully indoors on sunny window sills, although the bulbils of top onion and the bulbs of garlic will not develop to any extent. Pot clumps of chives in the fall, then leave them outside in freezing temperatures for about a month before you move them indoors to provide fresh chives through the winter. Plant top onion and garlic indoors at any time, using commercial potting soil. In seven to 10 days shoots will be visible; when they are 3 inches tall, garlic and top onion spears can be cut for use.

ALOE

A. vera, also called *A. barbadensis* (aloe, true aloe, bitter aloe, Barbados aloe)

Bitter aloe is a succulent perennial whose fleshly leaves contain a bitter yellow juice used in cosmetics and ointments for insect bites and sunburn. The thick, leathery, straplike green leaves grow to a length of 6 to 24 inches. They are usually edged with soft spines and, when young, are dotted with white spots. Old plants send up leafless blossom stalks that rise from the center of the rosettes of leaves to bear plumes of yellow or reddish bell-like flowers; however, pot-grown aloes rarely bloom.

HOW TO GROW. A semidesert plant, true aloe can be grown in the ground outdoors only in Zones 9 and 10. However, aloe grows easily anywhere in pots as a house plant or terrace plant. If kept on a terrace, the plant must be moved inside when the temperature drops below 50°. Aloe does best if it has four or more hours a day of direct sunlight, but it will grow fairly well in bright, indirect light.

Potted aloes need very little care: they thrive for years without repotting. Allow the soil to become fairly dry between thorough waterings. Overwatering in winter is hazardous; let the soil become quite dry between waterings.

Do not fertilize the first year after potting. Subsequently, feed once a year in the fall with standard house plant fertilizer diluted to half the strength recommended on the label; this increases the chance of flowering. The simplest way to propagate aloe is to detach the small rooted suckers that develop around its base, and then to plant these cuttings in pots of sandy soil.

ALOYSIA See *Lippia*

ALTHAEA

A. officinalis (marsh mallow)

Marsh mallow, a flowering perennial, takes its common name from the coastal marshes that are its natural habitat in Europe. Its tender leaves and tops are sometimes eaten as a salad green or cooked vegetable, but it is mainly grown for its decorative qualities. A relative of the hollyhock, marsh mallow has erect stems, 3 to 4 feet high, and pale pink to rose-colored flowers 1 to 1½ inches across. The flowers spring singly or in clusters from the axils of the upper leaves, and bloom in late summer. Marsh mallow's maple-like leaves are a velvety, soft gray-green with serrated edges.

HOW TO GROW. Marsh mallow grows in Zones 6–8. It does best in bright sun and a light, sandy, moist soil. Sow seeds indoors in the spring in flats, or outdoors in summer as soon as ripe seeds are available. When the seedlings are 2 to 3 inches high, thin or transplant them, spacing them 12 to 18 inches apart. For quicker results grow marsh mallow from root divisions in the spring. Use a sharp knife to divide the fleshy root to include a bud in each piece. If the fresh leaves and tops of the plant are to be eaten, harvest them before the plant flowers.

AMARACUS See *Origanum*
AMBROSIA See *Chenopodium*

ANCHUSA
A. officinalis (alkanet, bugloss)

Alkanet is a biennial bearing cucumber-tasting flowers that can be floated in wine punches and fruit cups for flavoring; the root bark provides a red dye. From midsummer until early fall, the 1- to 2-foot plant produces clusters of tiny blue, violet or purple blossoms. The hairy lancelike leaves, 3 to 6 inches long and 1 inch wide, are dark green and have a rough texture.

HOW TO GROW. Alkanet grows in Zones 6–10, although it may not survive the warm, humid winters of Florida and the Gulf Coast. It does best in full sun but tolerates partial shade. Provide good, well-drained soil supplemented with compost or manure. Plants can be started in the spring from seeds or root division, and in the fall from root cuttings. When started from seed, plants take a year to reach maturity. Sow the seeds about ¼ inch deep; when the seedlings are 1 to 2 inches high, transplant them about 12 inches apart. Cutting back the faded flowers encourages additional blossoming. In late fall, mulch the plants lightly—in moist climates, the pulpy roots are prone to rot under deep mulch.

To start plants from root cuttings, place 2-inch lengths upright in pots in commercial potting soil, covering the tips about 1 inch deep. Place the pots in a cold frame for the duration of the winter and set the new plants outdoors in the garden in the spring.

ANEMONE
A. pulsatilla, sometimes called *Pulsatilla vulgaris* (pasque flower, windflower)

Pasque flower is a low-growing, spring-flowering perennial, widely used for early bloom in northern rock gardens. Although it eventually reaches a height of 8 to 10 inches, the plant's first blossoms open barely above the soil. Each stem is topped by a cup-shaped blossom, 2 inches wide, in shades of blue, purple, pink, dull red or white accented by prominent yellow stamens. A fernlike leafy fringe surrounds the stem just below the flower, and more fernlike leaves arise from the root as the flowering season continues. The flowers are followed by fluffy white seed heads. All parts of this plant are covered with a delicate, hairlike growth that glistens in sunlight.

HOW TO GROW. Pasque flower thrives in the cool, moist areas of Zones 3–6; it will grow in sun or light shade, and does best in well-drained soil with a pH of 6.0 to 8.0. The easiest way to propagate pasque flower is from fresh seeds, gathered immediately after flowering. Sow them in seedbeds in late May or June, scattering them thinly so the plants will not be crowded. Transfer the young plants to permanent locations in the garden the following spring, setting them 8 to 12 inches apart.

ANETHUM
A. graveolens, also called *Peucedanum graveolens* (dill)

Dill is a tender annual with slightly sweet-tasting leaves that are used to flavor soups, vegetables, salads, sauces and

ALKANET
Anchusa officinalis

PASQUE FLOWER
Anemone pulsatilla

For climate zones and frost dates, see maps, pages 150–151.

DILL
Anethum graveolens

ANGELICA
Angelica archangelica

fish, and with pungent, somewhat bitter seeds that are used as an ingredient in pickles and in sauerkraut dishes. The threadlike blue-green leaves spread out in feathery branches from a hollow stalk 2 to 3 feet high. From June to October, if successive plantings are made, the plant produces umbrella clusters of tiny yellow flowers that ripen into small, thin seeds. One plant yields about ¼ cup of seeds, four to eight flower clusters and ½ cup of leaves.

HOW TO GROW. Dill grows outdoors in Zones 3–10, and can also be cultivated indoors as a pot plant. In the garden, it requires full sun and an acid soil—pH of 5.5 to 6.5—supplemented with compost or manure. Select a protected location; the hollow stalks, top-heavy with blossoms, can be easily knocked over by the wind. For summer and fall crops in Zones 3–8, sow seeds about twice a month from early spring to midsummer, setting them ¼ inch deep in rows 2 feet apart. For an early spring crop, sow seeds in the fall just before the ground freezes. In Zones 9 and 10 sow seeds from late summer through midwinter to have crops that mature in winter and spring. Thin the seedlings when they are about 2 inches high so the plants stand about 10 to 12 inches apart. (Transplanting is difficult because the root structure is so delicate.) If the plants appear weak when they reach a foot tall, scratch in 5-10-5 fertilizer at the rate of 3 ounces to a 10-foot row. The plants will be killed by the first frost, but self-sown seeds generally sprout to provide successive year's crops. Do not plant dill near fennel because this relative may cross-pollinate; the flavor of the resulting seeds and leaves is impossible to predict.

Dill grown indoors needs at least five hours a day of direct sunlight or 12 hours of bright artificial light. Fill 6-inch pots with potting soil moistened with lukewarm water. Scatter about six seeds over the surface. Wrap the pot in a clear plastic bag to keep the soil moist, and set it in a brightly lighted but not sunny place where the temperature is 65° to 75°. When true leaves appear, remove the plastic bag and place the pot in a sunny window. Keep the soil moist but not wet. When the plants reach a height of 3 to 4 inches, thin them to the three strongest plants in each pot. For a continuous supply of dill, plant two or three pots and alternate cuttings among them.

From indoor or outdoor plants, dill leaves can be cut any time and can be used fresh, dried or quick-frozen, although dried leaves lose most of their flavor. Fresh dill leaves should be finely chopped for flavoring. The seeds can be used fresh or dried. Separate the seeds from the flower heads by placing the cut stalks in a paper bag and shaking them; spread the seeds on a flat surface to dry, then store them in an airtight container.

ANGELICA
A. archangelica (angelica)

Angelica is a giant relative of parsley that towers 4 to 7 feet high. It is a biennial or short-lived perennial usually grown from summer-planted seed, but its life can be extended if the plant is prevented from flowering and bearing fruit. Every part of angelica is useful. Its somewhat bitter-tasting leaves are boiled and eaten like spinach or dried for medicinal teas. The thick, hollow stalk can be boiled like rhubarb but is most often candied and used as a flavoring in pastries, cakes, candies and desserts. The juniper-flavored seeds can be substituted for real juniper berries in making gin; oil from the roots flavors various liqueurs; and dried roots are ground for sachets.

In the first year angelica produces leaves but no stalk, and it seldom grows more than 2 to 3 feet high. In the second year, or sometimes the third, the plant shoots up a flower stalk to its full dramatic height and is capped in early summer with clusters of greenish-white flowers called umbels, which are followed by ½-inch straw-textured yellow fruit, each containing a single ¼-inch brown seed. If the stalk is cut before flowers form, the plant lives another year; if the flowers are allowed to go to seed, the plant dies, but seedlings will appear in the garden.

HOW TO GROW. Angelica grows in Zones 3–6 and does best in moist, slightly acid loam with a pH of 6.5 to 7.0. Plant it in a cool, partially shaded location. It is ordinarily raised from seed, but plant the seeds ¼ inch deep immediately after they ripen, because they quickly lose their germinating ability. If they must be held until the following spring, store them in a refrigerator. Sow a pinch of seeds where you want them to grow at 2½- to 3-foot intervals. When they germinate about three weeks later, thin to leave only the strongest plant at each site. Although seedlings can be transplanted, mature plants cannot. If the stalks are cut back in the second year, the roots will send up new shoots that can be transplanted. Roots intended for use as flavoring should be dug during the fall of the first year, when they are tenderest. The leaves and stalks should be harvested during the second year; the stalks should be cut during the spring before the flowers begin to open.

ANISE See *Pimpinella*
ANISE FERN See *Myrrhis*
ANISE HYSSOP See *Agastache*

ANTHEMIS

A. nobilis (chamomile, Roman chamomile)

This aromatic, low-growing perennial makes a soft, lush ground cover long used as a grass substitute in the lawns of Europe. It can be mowed and is drought resistant. The whole plant has a pleasantly pungent fragrance. The stems lie flat and creep along the ground, rooting as they go, creating a feathery gray-green mat 3 to 10 inches high, depending upon the fertility of the soil. During midsummer, flower stems rise 12 to 14 inches high and bear ¾-inch white daisy-like blossoms. The oil of chamomile blossoms has found many uses, from a rinse for lightening and softening the hair to a flavoring for sherry.

HOW TO GROW. Chamomile grows in Zones 3–10 in almost any well-drained soil. Though it will tolerate some shade, it does best in full sun. Plants are most easily propagated from root divisions, taken in the fall or early spring. To grow from seed, sow indoors in midwinter on a sunny window sill and transplant to individual pots when the first true leaves appear. Set the new plants outdoors in the spring, as close as 4 inches apart for ground cover, 8 and 10 inches apart for row planting. Keep the soil moist but not soggy until the plants are well established.

ANTHRISCUS

A. cerefolium (chervil, beaked parsley, French parsley)

Chervil, one of the *fines herbes* of French cooking, is an annual grown for its anise- or parsley-flavored leaves, which intensify the flavors of other herbs. It is a member of the parsley family and its lacy leaves resemble those of parsley, but are a lighter green and more feathery. Within eight weeks after planting, chervil produces umbrella-shaped clusters of small white blossoms on a 1½- to 2-foot-tall hollow stem. The flowers quickly ripen into slender black seeds. By cutting back the flower heads before they bloom, you can stimulate new leaf growth. Each plant produces about ¼ cup

CHAMOMILE
Anthemis nobilis

CHERVIL
Anthriscus cerefolium

of leaves at the first harvest, and somewhat less than that on subsequent cuttings.

HOW TO GROW. Chervil can be grown outdoors in Zones 3–10, and can be grown indoors as a pot plant. It grows best in partial shade and a light, moist garden soil, pH 6.0 to 7.0, supplemented with compost or manure. It is harmed by hot weather and high humidity, and it does not easily survive transplanting. Seeds can be sown at any time of the year, but they germinate best in cool weather; sow them at three- to four-week intervals from early spring until late fall. In warm climates, sow seeds in late summer and fall for winter and spring harvests. Press the seeds lightly into the soil, and when the seedlings are 3 to 4 inches high, thin them to stand 6 to 9 inches apart. Plants that are left to flower will reseed themselves, and a few plants should be permitted to bloom for this purpose.

Chervil grown indoors in pots does best with four or five hours a day of direct sunlight or 12 hours of strong artificial light. It thrives in cool temperatures, under 60°. Fill 6-inch pots with commercial potting soil, moistened with lukewarm water. Sprinkle a few seeds on the surface. Slip the pot into a clear plastic bag and set it away from direct sunlight in a place where the temperature is 50° to 60°. When plants appear, remove the plastic bag and place the pot in a sunny window. Keep the soil moist. When the plants are 1 to 2 inches high, remove all but three in each pot.

Fresh harvests can be made from chervil plants at one-month intervals if only the top leaves are removed each time. Such pinching back will encourage new growth. Harvest chervil leaves for drying or for freezing at a point before the flowers open.

APPLE MINT See *Mentha*

ARMORACIA

A. rusticana, also called *Cochlearia armoracia* (horseradish)

Horseradish is a hardy perennial cultivated for its sharp-tasting white root, which is grated or ground for a table condiment. The plant's coarse, wavy leaves spread outward in a radius of 2 to 3 feet, and in summer a slender stalk bearing small, faintly scented white flowers rises to a height of 3 feet. The tiny fruit pods usually fail to mature, so horseradish is always propagated from root cuttings. Thick, white and long-lived, the taproot reaches deep into the soil, and its numerous branching side roots and suckers make the plant difficult to remove from the garden once it is established. Six plants will yield enough horseradish for an average family.

HOW TO GROW. Horseradish, hardy in Zones 3–10, will grow in any moist garden soil that is supplemented with manure or compost but kept relatively neutral with a pH of about 7.0. Work the soil to a depth of 2 feet before planting. Plant 4- to 5-inch root cuttings in the fall, spacing the segments 10 to 15 inches apart and setting them in the ground at a slant or vertically, thick ends up, so that the top of each cutting is 3 to 4 inches below ground level. Firm the soil well after planting. In late spring, dig around each plant and carefully rub off the side roots to insure a well-formed taproot. By all means, do not dig the plants up to remove these side roots; horseradish is delicate and can be easily damaged if it is handled roughly.

To harvest, dig up the root in the late fall, when it is tastiest, and store it in cool, moist sand until needed. Alternatively, the root can be grated immediately and preserved in distilled or white wine vinegar, or it can be dried and ground into powder for reconstituting with water.

HORSERADISH
Armoracia rusticana

ARTEMISIA

A. absinthium (wormwood); *A. dracunculus* (tarragon, estragon, French tarragon)

Though of the same genus, these two artemisias differ greatly in personality. Wormwood is one of the "bitter herbs" of the Bible; it was once used as a flavoring in absinthe, the notorious French liqueur whose constant use was said to derange the mind. Tarragon is one of the essential herbs of French cooking; the subtle anise flavor of its leaves complements beef, veal, chicken, fish and eggs and provides the distinctive ingredient in tarragon vinegar. Tarragon's use is solely culinary but wormwood is also used in the preparation of a muscle liniment.

Both plants are perennials with tough, slender stems that may become somewhat woody and have a habit of sprawling late in the summer. Wormwood grown in home gardens as an ornament becomes 2 to 4 feet high and has deep-cut silvery-gray leaves. Both leaves and stems are covered with downy hairs, giving the plant a delicate chalky appearance that contrasts with the greens of other plants in the garden. In midsummer, small greenish-yellow blossoms appear. Both the leaves and flowers have a pungent odor.

Tarragon grows 24 to 36 inches tall and its leaves are long, narrow and dark green. In midsummer tiny greenish-white flowers bloom but they never set seeds; consequently tarragon can only be grown from cuttings or root divisions. A mature tarragon plant will produce about 2 cups of fresh leaves at the first cutting, less at subsequent harvests.

HOW TO GROW. Wormwood, hardy in Zones 3–10, thrives in sun or partial shade and in almost any soil. It can be raised from seed, which germinates best when planted in the fall, but it is usually started in the early spring from root divisions. It can also be propagated from stem cuttings taken in early summer. Set seedlings, rooted stem cuttings or root divisions 1½ to 2 feet apart, to allow for the plant's spreading habit. Tall stems can be staked or they can be trimmed back. In the fall, cut back the plants to the ground in areas where the soil freezes and cover with a light mulch of salt hay or straw after the ground has frozen.

Tarragon is hardy in Zones 5–10 but is difficult to grow in the warmer climate of Florida and the Gulf Coast. It does best in full sun and a well-drained, slightly sandy soil with a pH of 6.0 to 7.5. Start with root divisions or rooted stem cuttings; tarragon seeds sold commercially are usually Russian tarragon, a less flavorful variety of the genus. Set plants in the ground in the early spring, 18 to 24 inches apart. In early summer, after cutting the first crop of leaves, scratch a handful of 5-10-5 fertilizer into the soil around the base of each plant. Tarragon is apt to die over the winter if grown in cold, wet soil; the best precaution is a well-drained site and plenty of space between plants. In northern areas it should also be mulched with salt hay or straw. Apply the mulch after the ground is frozen solid. Every three or four years, dig up the tarragon in the spring, when the plant is 2 or 3 inches high, and divide the roots into several smaller clumps for transplanting.

Tarragon can be cut for flavoring at any time. To dry leaves for winter use, cut the stems 3 inches from the ground in early summer and again in early fall. Lay them flat or hang them in loose bunches in a dark, airy place; when dry, crumble the leaves and store in an airtight container.

Tarragon grown indoors needs at least five hours of direct sunlight a day. Use any commercial potting soil. Pot tarragon for indoor use no later than midsummer; most tarragon potted later dies even if temperatures are warm and light conditions are excellent.

WORMWOOD
Artemisia absinthium

TARRAGON
Artemisia dracunculus

For climate zones and frost dates, see maps, pages 150–151.

WOODRUFF
Asperula odorata

ORACH
Atriplex hortensis

ASPERULA

A. odorata (woodruff, sweet woodruff)

Sweet woodruff, a low-growing perennial 6 to 8 inches high, is unique in having leaves that smell of new-mown hay—but only when dried. The leaves are used to flavor wine punches, especially May wine, and they are also used in herb teas and sachets. Sweet woodruff long was used as a strewing herb, releasing its sweet fragrance as it was walked upon. The plant has shiny oblong leaves growing in delicate whorls around the stem. In late April and May it is capped with clusters of tiny white star-shaped flowers that are excellent for cutting. An attractive ground cover uniquely suitable for shady areas, it spreads rapidly from creeping above-ground roots called stolons. Its seeds are thickly covered with hairy bristles that attach themselves to the fur and feathers of animals and birds.

HOW TO GROW. Sweet woodruff grows best in Zones 4–8. It needs shade and a loose, moist, acid soil—pH 4.5 to 5.5—supplemented with leaf mold. In its natural European habitat it is a woodland plant and in gardens it will turn brown and die if exposed to full sun and dry soil. Seeds germinate well if fresh, but old seeds must often be in the ground about a year before they sprout; for this reason root divisions or stem cuttings are the common methods of propagation. Take cuttings from mature plants in the spring or fall and set them in wet sand; they will root in three weeks or less. Make root divisions in the spring or early fall and set the root clumps in the ground 9 to 12 inches apart. Soak the soil well after planting and keep it moist but not soggy.

Sweet woodruff is harvested in late spring, just before it blooms or while it is still in flower, when its new-mown-hay smell is most intense. Dry in a cool, dark place so the leaves retain some greenness, then strip the leaves from the stem and store them in an airtight container.

Sweet woodruff can be potted in the summer and taken indoors. It requires a moist but well-drained acid soil, cool conditions and at least five hours of filtered sunlight.

ATRIPLEX

A. hortensis (orach, sea purslane, French spinach)

Orach is a tall, erect annual that shoots up to a height of 5 to 6 feet in a single season. The arrowhead-shaped leaves, up to 5 inches long and sprinkled with a crystalline substance, are sometimes eaten as a spinach substitute. However, it is chiefly grown at the back of an annual border for its ornamental foliage. The variety *A. hortensis rubra* has deep red leaves, an effective contrast with green foliage both in the garden and in flower arrangements. In summer, orach bears inconspicuous flowers on short stalks that grow along the main stem.

HOW TO GROW. Orach needs full sun and grows in any light, well-drained soil. The plant survives in dry soil, but the leaves are most edible if the soil is kept moist enough to produce succulent growth. Sow the seeds ¼ to ½ inch deep as early in the spring as the ground can be worked. Thin the seedlings so that the plants stand 8 to 12 inches apart. If seeds are to be saved, gather them just before the pods open so they do not blow away. Orach seeds itself readily, and therefore some gardeners consider it to be a weed.

B

BALM, LEMON or **SWEET** See *Melissa*

BAPTISIA

B. tinctoria (wild indigo, yellow false indigo, shoo-fly)

Wild indigo was cultivated in America in colonial times for

the pale blue dye provided by its woody stems. Some farmers also tied bunches of the plant to the harnesses of their horses in the belief that it kept insects away; hence, it came to be known as shoo-fly. A 2- to 3-foot-tall, broadly branching perennial, the plant has stems with ¾- to 1-inch, silverygreen, clover-shaped leaves. When the plant is two or three years old, it begins to produce 1½- to 3-inch spikes of small pea-like yellow blossoms. It blooms continuously from midto late summer. Wild indigo is often used as a cut flower and as a border plant in the drier sections of wild gardens. Young shoots resemble those of asparagus and can be substituted for that herb as a pottage.

HOW TO GROW. Yellow false indigo can be grown in Zones 3–10 in almost any soil. It tolerates light shade, but flowers most abundantly in full sun. Sow seeds in the garden at any time, covering them with soil twice the thickness of the seed. Or start them in pots in a cold frame, four seeds to a 6-inch pot. Thin or transplant the seedlings before they are 1 foot high, setting them 18 to 30 inches apart. Wild indigoes almost never need dividing; although the clumps increase in size, taproots reach deep into the ground instead of spreading out to encroach upon the roots of nearby plants.

BARBADOS ALOE. See *Aloe*

BARBAREA
B. vulgaris (winter cress, upland cress, yellow rocket)

This hardy biennial member of the mustard family has the unusual habit of growing vigorously during winter months whenever there is a warm spell. The young lower leaves are a somewhat bitter winter substitute for watercress, and can be cooked like spinach as a vegetable. Uncooked leaves can be used as salad greens.

Winter cress grows from 1 to 2 feet tall with erect, branching stems. From April through August it produces dense clusters of tiny yellow flowers. The flowers are followed by thin, pencil-shaped seed pods an inch in length. Leaves are bright green and glossy.

HOW TO GROW. Winter cress grows in Zones 3–7. Sow seeds in the fall in rich, moist garden soil. To harvest seeds, remove the pods in late summer as soon as they begin to dry. If the pods split open, the seeds will fall and germinate nearby. Winter cress can also be propagated from root divisions and cuttings made in the spring. Lower leaves can be harvested for eating from late autumn through early spring as often as they appear.

BASIL See *Ocimum*
BAY See *Laurus*
BEAKED PARSLEY See *Anthriscus*
BEDSTRAW, YELLOW See *Galium*
BEE BALM See *Monarda*
BEE BREAD See *Borago*
BELGIAN ENDIVE See *Cichorium*
BENNE See *Sesamum*
BERGAMOT See *Monarda*
BETONY, ST. PAUL'S See *Veronica*
BETONY, WOOD or WOOLLY See *Stachys*
BIBLE LEAF See *Chrysanthemum*
BIRD'S FOOT See *Trigonella*
BISHOP'S WORT See *Stachys*
BITTER ALOE See *Aloe*
BITTER BUTTONS See *Tanacetum*
BITTER WINTER CRESS See *Barbarea*
BLACK CUMIN See *Nigella*
BLACK THYME See *Thymus*

WILD INDIGO
Baptisia tinctoria

WINTER CRESS
Barbarea vulgaris

For climate zones and frost dates, see maps, pages 150–151.

BORAGE
Borago officinalis

WHITE MUSTARD
Brassica alba

BLACKWORT See *Symphytum*
BLESSED THISTLE See *Cnicus*
BLOODWORT See *Geranium*
BONESET See *Symphytum*

BORAGO

B. officinalis (borage, bee bread, star flower)

An annual reaching 1 to 2 feet tall, borage has cool, cucumber-tasting leaves used to flavor salads, cream-cheese spreads and tall summer drinks; its sky blue, white or occasionally pink flowers are floated on punches or candied for desserts. Both the leaves and stems of borage are covered with fine hairs that become woolly and rough as the plant ages; therefore only fresh young leaves and stems, finely chopped, are used for flavoring. The star-shaped flowers, which bloom from spring to midsummer, attract bees, hence the name bee bread. Because the flowers are pendulous, borage is often planted high on a slope so the drooping heads will be visible.

HOW TO GROW. Borage, grown in Zones 3–10, requires full sun and does best in infertile, relatively light, dry soil with a pH of 6.0 to 7.0. Sow the seeds in the garden in the fall or very early spring, ⅛ to ¼ inch deep, where they are to grow, because borage is difficult to transplant successfully except when very small. When the seedlings are 2 to 3 inches high, thin them to stand 10 to 12 inches apart. Keep the soil moist while the plants are young. Borage seeds will keep up to eight years. Plants seed themselves readily, coming up year after year without attention.

BRASSICA

B. alba, also known as *Sinapis alba* (white mustard, yellow mustard)

The white mustard plant, a 10- to 24-inch-tall annual topped with clusters of bright yellow flowers, spreads so readily it can be a nuisance. It is cultivated commercially for the pale yellow seeds, which are crushed to make table mustard; so many seeds are required, however, that it is impracticable for home gardeners to grow it for this purpose. Young mustard leaves make a peppery flavoring for salad and are widely cooked as greens.

The bright green leaves of the mustard plant reach a length of 8 inches, decreasing in size as they ascend the stem; the four-petaled yellow flowers that cluster at the top are each about ½ inch across. The seed pod contains four to eight seeds, each about ¹/₁₆ inch wide.

HOW TO GROW. White mustard does best in full sun and will grow in almost any well-drained soil. Sow seeds in early spring or late summer; the plants will be large enough to harvest in approximately two months. If grown during midsummer, the foliage is too strong for most tastes. Mustard greens can also be grown indoors to be eaten as seedlings; sow them in a shallow container of potting soil. When the seedlings are 1 to 2 inches tall, cut them off close to the soil.

BUGLE or BUGLEWEED See *Ajuga*
BUGLOSS See *Anchusa*
BURNET, SALAD See *Sanguisorba*
BURNING BUSH See *Dictamnus*

C

CALAMONDIN ORANGE See *Citrus*
CALAMUS See *Acorus*

CALENDULA

C. officinalis (calendula, pot marigold)

Few plants are easier to grow than the calendula, an annual that is one of the most decorative of all herbs. It reaches 12 to 18 inches in height and produces orange or yellow flowers; the petals are used for food coloring and as an inexpensive substitute for saffron. The furry stems are clasped by dark-green leaves that may be 6 inches long. All summer the brilliant flowers, 2 to 4 inches across, open in the early morning and close at dusk. They are striking in a flower bed and in flower arrangements.

HOW TO GROW. Calendulas grow almost anywhere in almost any soil, although they do best in rich, loamy soil; they need full sun. In Zones 2–7, sow seeds outdoors as soon as the soil can be worked in the spring, covering them with ½ inch of soil. In Zones 8–10, a late summer or early fall sowing will provide winter and spring flowers. When seedlings are 4 to 6 inches high, thin or transplant them to stand 10 to 12 inches apart. Calendula plants blossom continuously from late spring through early frosts. To encourage continuous flowering, nip off dead blossoms before they mature into seed.

To harvest calendula petals, strip them from the newly opened flowers and use them fresh or dried. To dry them, lay them on paper in a cool, dark, airy room so they do not touch one another, and turn them frequently. When the petals are crisp, store in an airtight container.

To grow calendula indoors, sow seeds outdoors in midsummer and transplant seedlings to 6-inch pots filled with commercial potting soil. Bring plants indoors to a sunny window sill before severe frost. They do best with night temperatures at 50°, daytime readings of 60° to 65°. Keep the soil barely moist; if it is allowed to become soggy, the roots may rot. Plants require at least five hours of direct sunlight or 12 hours of strong artificial light.

CAMOMILE See *Anthemis*
CARAWAY See *Carum*
CARDOON See *Cynara*

CARTHAMUS
C. tinctorius (safflower, saffron thistle, false saffron)

An annual 2 to 3 feet tall, safflower bears colorful flowers that are used as a substitute for saffron and as a red-to-yellow dye for coloring foods, textiles and cosmetics (it is a principal ingredient of rouge). The dried seed heads are also useful in winter bouquets. Oil extracted from its seeds is a popular salad oil, since it is the polyunsaturated type called for in many diets.

The dark green leaves are spiny, and the 1-inch ball-like flowers, which bloom in midsummer, have deep yellow florets that deepen into orange as the season progresses. The flowers are followed by toothlike white seeds, source of the oil, which ripen by the end of summer.

HOW TO GROW. Safflower can be grown anywhere, provided it does not get much summer rain, which tends to spread disease among its leaves and to cause newly ripened seeds to germinate while still on the stalk. It does best in the dry climate of the West. It needs full sun, thrives in poor, light, dry soil, and re-seeds itself. Sow seeds ¼ inch deep in the spring, when all danger of frost has passed. Put them where the plants are to remain, since safflower is hard to transplant. Seedlings should be thinned to stand 4 to 6 inches apart. Until the prickly spines develop, the tender leaves and stems are appealing to rabbits, so protect the young plants with wire fencing. Cut and dry the flower heads in late summer to make the saffron-like powder for use in cooking; store the dried petals in an airtight container and powder them as they are needed.

CALENDULA
Calendula officinalis

SAFFLOWER
Carthamus tinctorius

For climate zones and frost dates, see maps, pages 150–151.

CARAWAY
Carum carvi

CARUM
C. carvi (caraway)

Caraway is most often grown for its seeds, which contribute a licorice-like flavor in many German and Austrian recipes for cakes, cookies, breads and liqueurs. But the feathery leaves, resembling carrot tops, and the long, pale-yellow taproots are also cooked and eaten as vegetables. A hardy biennial, caraway produces only a 6- to 8-inch mound of leaves the first year; the following spring, a thin flower stalk shoots up 2 to 3 feet, bearing flat clusters of tiny off-white flowers that ripen into ¼-inch brown crescent-shaped seeds. When the seeds mature, the plant dies. One plant produces about four clusters, each with about one tablespoon of seeds. Caraway often seeds itself if seed heads are not harvested before they break open.

HOW TO GROW. Caraway can be cultivated from Zones 3–10, but it does not do well in southern Florida and along the Gulf Coast because of the hot, rainy, humid summer. It will grow in almost any well-drained soil with a pH of 6.0 to 7.0, but it needs full sun. Plant in the fall or early spring, sowing seeds ⅛ inch deep in rows 2 feet apart. Germination is slow except when seeds are sown fresh, immediately after harvesting. When seedlings reach a height of 2 inches, thin plants to stand 6 to 12 inches apart. Plants do best if they are not transplanted.

To harvest caraway seeds, cut seed heads off in midsummer as soon as the seeds turn brown; if they are left on the plant until thoroughly dry, they will scatter. Seeds to be used in cooking should be scalded immediately after picking to kill any insects that may be in the seeds. Scald the fresh-picked seeds in boiling water; then dry them in the sun for several days, bringing them inside at night. When dry, store them in an airtight jar. Seeds intended for future planting should not be scalded because the heat kills the seed embryos.

CASSIA
C. marilandica (wild senna)

Wild senna is a dramatic 4- to 7-foot-tall perennial, grown for the fernlike foliage and yellow blossoms that make it a striking addition to the back border of any herb garden. Opposing pairs of delicate light-green leaflets make up each 6- to 10-inch leaf. Throughout the summer, ½-inch blossoms cluster at the top of the stems, their yellow petals framing conspicuous dark brown or purplish anthers. After the petals have fallen, 4-inch-long flat pods develop.

HOW TO GROW. Wild senna grows in Zones 4–10 in full sun or light shade and in any well-drained soil. To propagate, take seeds from the dry pods in the fall and sow them where the plants are to grow. Thin seedlings to stand 2 feet apart. Once established, wild senna can remain undisturbed for an indefinite period.

CATMINT or CATNIP See *Nepeta*
CHAMOMILE See *Anthemis*
CHAMOMILE, GERMAN See *Matricaria*
CHEESE RENNET See *Galium*

CHENOPODIUM
C. bonus-henricus (Good-King-Henry, English mercury); *C. botrys* (ambrosia, Jerusalem oak, feather geranium)

These two chenopodia are grown for very different purposes. Good-King-Henry, a 12- to 30-inch-tall perennial, is a potherb; its large, bright green, arrowhead-shaped leaves, 2 to 4½ inches long, are cooked as a substitute for its relative, spinach. In addition, the young shoots of the plant can be cut and eaten like asparagus when they are about the thickness

WILD SENNA
Cassia marilandica

of a finger. Ambrosia, on the other hand, is a hardy annual grown for its intensely fragrant foliage and flowers and for its elegant arching stems, which are valued in dried flower arrangements. Ambrosia's ½- to 2-inch-long leaves are red on the underside, dark green on top, and resemble oak leaves in shape. When the plant reaches its full height of 2 to 3 feet, sprays of tiny yellowish-green flowers without petals bloom in elongated clusters over most of the stems, bending the stems with their weight into graceful plumes.

HOW TO GROW. Good-King-Henry can be grown in Zones 5–8; ambrosia in Zones 3–10. Both flourish in any kind of well-drained soil, but ambrosia does best in full sun while Good-King-Henry is better grown in partial shade. To propagate Good-King-Henry from seed, sow the seeds in spring, then thin the seedlings, which will be slow to appear, to stand 9 to 12 inches apart. Feed during the growing season with any vegetable-garden fertilizer; new plants can be obtained more easily by dividing the root clumps of mature plants. Until the plants are three years old, cut only a few leaves at a time to avoid injuring the plant. They taste best in the spring. If early shoots are to be cut like asparagus, cover the plant roots with 4 to 5 inches of leaf mold or compost in the fall, shielding them from light to ensure that the spring shoots will be blanched white and tender. Cut the shoots off just beneath the soil's surface.

To plant ambrosia, scatter the tiny seeds on top of the soil in spring or fall where you want the plants to grow, and thin the seedlings to stand 12 inches apart. Harvest the plant for dried arrangements before it goes to seed; cut stems and place them in vases without water to dry in a place sheltered from the sun. The graceful dried sprays retain a delicate green hue. Left unharvested, ambrosia will reproduce itself from fallen seeds and can become weedy. It has become naturalized in waste places throughout most of the United States and southern Canada.

CHERRY PIE See *Heliotropium*
CHERVIL See *Anthriscus*
CHERVIL, GIANT See *Myrrhis*
CHICORY See *Cichorium*
CHINESE PARSLEY See *Coriandrum*
CHIVE See *Allium*

CHRYSANTHEMUM
C. balsamita tanacetoides (costmary, alecost, Bible leaf)

The fragrance of mint, lemon and balsam seems pleasingly combined in the oval leaves of costmary, a sprawling perennial growing 2 to 3 feet tall. The dried leaves add fragrance to potpourris and serve as a fixative to preserve the other scents. When young, the leaves can be included in salads, though they taste rather bitter. They were once used as a flavoring for beer, hence the name alecost. The herbalist Gerard noted the beneficial effects of a conserve made from costmary leaves and sugar, which "doth warm and dry the braine and openeth the stoppings of the same."

Most of the 5- to 8-inch-long leaves spread from the base of the plant. In late summer, tiny, bright yellow, button flowers appear without the raylike petals characteristic of other *balsamita* varieties.

HOW TO GROW. Costmary, grown in Zones 6–9, needs full sun and dry, well-drained soil. It can be grown in partial shade but then rarely flowers. Because costmary spreads rapidly from underground stolons or runners, it is easier to start new plants from root divisions than from seed. Set young plants in the garden in early spring, placing them 2 to 3 feet apart to allow for their sprawling growth.

GOOD-KING-HENRY
Chenopodium bonus-henricus

AMBROSIA
Chenopodium botrys

COSTMARY
Chrysanthemum balsamita tanacetoides

For climate zones and frost dates, see maps, pages 150–151.

107

To grow costmary indoors, transplant a root division into commercial potting soil in a 4- to 6-inch pot. Keep it in a sunny window. The soil should be moist but not soggy. Indoors it seldom grows more than 18 inches high.

CHRYSANTHEMUM See *Tanacetum*
CHURCH STEEPLES See *Agrimonia*
CICELY, SWEET See *Myrrhis*

CICHORIUM
C. intybus (chicory, succory, witloof chicory, Belgian endive)

Chicory is best known for the flavor of its ground and roasted taproot, which adds distinction to the coffee blend popular in New Orleans. But in the herb garden, throughout the summer the 3- to 6-foot-tall perennial produces lovely light blue, pink or white daisy-like flowers along its lanky stem. The blossoms open and close like clockwork, morning and evening; in fact, their timing is so reliable that the botanist Linnaeus included chicory in a floral clock that marked hours with blooms.

HOW TO GROW. Chicory, hardy in Zones 3–10, needs full sun and will grow in almost any soil. In fact, in some areas it is a roadside weed. Turn over the soil to a depth of at least 1 foot to accommodate the long taproot, and dig in generous amounts of manure or compost. Sow the seeds in early spring, covering them with ¼ to ½ inch of soil. When the first true leaves appear, thin the seedlings to stand about 1 foot apart. Chicory does not flower the first year, but blossoms appear during the second and succeeding years.

Special strains of chicory are grown as gourmet vegetables under the names of witloof chicory and Belgian endive. Their cultivation takes two stages. In the fall of the first year, just before the ground has frozen, trim back the top growth to ground level, dig up the root and bury it at least 10 inches deep in a large box of sand, which is then placed in a cool, dark place. Keep the sand moist but not soggy, and in three or four weeks a huge tightly furled bud of creamy-white foliage will sprout from the top of the root; this part may be cooked whole or separated into leaves for use as a green in salads.

CILANTRO See *Coriandrum*

CITRUS
C. mitis (calamondin orange)

This miniature fruit tree, a subtropical evergreen native to the Philippines, is widely cultivated in America as an ornamental house plant. When tub grown it rarely reaches a height of more than 2 feet, and can be kept inside year round or can be moved outside during the warmer months. Intermittently throughout the year, calamondin orange produces a succession of fragrant, ⅓- to 1-inch white flowers followed by fruit that requires nearly a year to ripen. The ripened fruit, about 1 inch in diameter, is edible, albeit somewhat tart; it makes a good marmalade.

HOW TO GROW. Calamondin orange grows best in slightly acid soil with a pH of 6.0 to 6.5, and can be raised outdoors where winter temperatures do not fall below 20°; below 50°, however, the plant becomes dormant.

In Zones 3–8 it must be treated as a pot plant and can be kept outdoors only during the summer months. It can be started from seed, but is best propagated from stem cuttings taken from midsummer to late fall. For the most abundant flowers and fruit, place the potted plant in a location that receives at least four hours of direct sunlight a day, and has night temperatures of 50° to 55° and day temperatures of 68°

CHICORY
Cichorium intybus

CALAMONDIN ORANGE
Citrus mitis

to 72°. Calamondin orange is damaged by overwatering, but the roots must never be allowed to become completely dry. It thrives in a moist atmosphere and should be set in a tray of pebbles that is kept filled with water to supply the needed humidity. If a plant becomes too large, cut it back as severely as necessary; pruning is best done in the early spring. Calamondin orange, like other citrus species, is vulnerable to attack from mealy bugs and spider mites. To control the insects, wash the plants with a forceful spray of water and, if this is not effective, spray them with malathion every 10 days as necessary—but do not spray with malathion indoors.

CLORINDA GERANIUM See *Pelargonium*

CNICUS
C. benedictus (blessed thistle)

Blessed thistle, a 2-foot-tall ornamental annual, has 2- to 6-inch-long silvery-green leaves, sometimes blotched with milky white, which are edged with sharp spines. Throughout the summer, each hairy stem ends in a tousled yellow flower head, about an inch across, surrounded with bristly yellow bracts and a circle of leaves.

HOW TO GROW. Blessed thistle flourishes in Zones 3–10 and grows in sun or shade in any well-drained or dry soil. Sow seeds in late spring, either in the garden or indoors in a box of potting soil. Thin seedlings or transplant them to stand 18 to 24 inches apart.

COCHLEARIA See *Armoracia*
COCKLEBUR See *Agrimonia*
COLTSFOOT See *Tussilago*
COMFREY See *Symphytum*

CORIANDRUM
C. sativum (coriander, Chinese parsley, cilantro)

The aromatic lemony seeds of coriander are used in baking and as a curry spice, and its dainty parsley-like leaves add pungency to Chinese, Middle Eastern and Latin American cooking. The plant is an annual that becomes 1 to 2 feet tall. In summer the delicately branched stems bear lacy flower heads of tiny white, pale pink or lavender blossoms, which ripen into small light-brown fruit about ⅛ inch in diameter. A coriander plant will produce enough fruit for ¼ cup of seeds in two months, or, if flower heads are removed, ½ cup of leaves.

HOW TO GROW. Coriander grows from Zones 3–10, but does best in dry climates; it can be raised only with difficulty in Florida and along the Gulf Coast because of the hot, humid, rainy summers. It requires full sun and will grow in any well-drained soil of average richness. Sow seeds in the late spring when the danger of frost has passed, in a location protected from the wind—coriander becomes top-heavy and tends to blow over. Plant seeds ½ to ¾ inch deep. When seedlings are 2 to 3 inches tall, thin to stand 8 to 10 inches apart. Plants started in spring will bloom about nine weeks later and produce seeds in midsummer. If the fruit is allowed to ripen on the plant, coriander will seed itself.

Coriander leaves can be cut for seasoning as soon as the plant is 4 to 6 inches tall; they are always used fresh. Harvest coriander seeds as soon as the fruit is light brown. Cut off the entire plant with the seed pods still attached and carefully drop it into a paper bag; dry in a warm, dark place. Shake the dried fruits inside the bag to remove them from the stems, then rub the dried fruit between the palms of the hands to split the pods and remove the seeds. Store seeds in an airtight container.

BLESSED THISTLE
Cnicus benedictus

CORIANDER
Coriandrum sativum

For climate zones and frost dates, see maps, pages 150–151.

SAMPHIRE
Crithmum maritimum

SAFFRON CROCUS
Crocus sativus

CRITHMUM

C. maritimum (samphire, sea fennel)

Samphire, a salt-resistant perennial, is native to an area where few plants survive, in the high winds and sea spray of the beaches and coastal cliffs of southern and western Europe. Its rubbery, 1-inch leaves are divided into narrow, spear-shaped leaflets that are salty, aromatic and rich in iodine; they are sometimes pickled as a relish or are eaten fresh in a salad.

The plant reaches a height of 9 to 12 inches. In early summer samphire produces small clusters of flower heads.

HOW TO GROW. Samphire needs full sun and well-drained rocky or sandy soil. It grows in Zones 6–10, but must be protected against freezing with a mulch of leaves. Sow seeds in early spring, as soon as the soil can be prepared, and thin the plants to stand 18 inches apart. Samphire can also be propagated by root division in the spring or from stem cuttings. If seaweed is available, use as a mulch around plants or dig in a spoonful of table salt once or twice during the growing season.

CROCUS

C. sativus (saffron crocus)

This fall-flowering bulb plant has been cultivated since ancient times for saffron, the flavoring derived from its flower stigma, a substance so rare it was long considered a prerogative of royalty. It takes roughly 8,000 flowers to produce 3½ ounces of dried saffron. Nero ordered saffron to be sprinkled on the streets of Rome for his entry into the city, and medieval scribes burnished saffron upon foil as a substitute for gold in illuminated manuscripts. Still cultivated in parts of Europe and Asia as a coloring and flavoring agent for food, the plant is grown mostly for garden decoration in the United States and is prized because it blooms in the fall, when most flowers are gone.

Saffron crocus grows from a small brown bulbous corm, about 1 inch in diameter, from which rise several stems 3 to 4 inches high. The stems produce sweetly scented chalice-shaped buds. Each bud opens to a star-shaped flower about 2½ inches across, which stays open at night as well as during the day. Grasslike leaves, about 18 inches long, appear with the flower in the fall and stay green through the winter, dying back in late spring.

HOW TO GROW. Saffron crocus grows in Zones 5–10 but does best in Zones 5–7 where winters are cold. It tolerates light shade, but does best in full sun in a sheltered location and a light, rich, well-drained soil. Plant corms as early as they are available, placing them in groups 2 to 6 inches apart; cover them with 2 to 4 inches of soil. Left undisturbed, they multiply naturally and increase in beauty from one year to the next, though they can be dug up and divided in early summer every three or four years, if desired. Saffron crocus is sterile, and can be propagated only by proliferation of the underground corms.

CUMINUM

C. cyminum, also called *C. odorum* (cumin)

Cumin is a Mediterranean annual cultivated for its pungent seeds, which have been prized as a condiment since Biblical times, and are today an ingredient of Indian, North

African and Mexican cooking. The plant's diminutive size, 4 to 6 inches, and spidery, deep-green foliage make it a useful edging plant. The rose-colored or white blossoms are tiny, but mature into the yellowish-brown seeds, about ¼ inch long, which must be dried to develop their distinctive flavor similar to caraway.

HOW TO GROW. Cumin needs three to four months of warm summer weather to mature. It is grown in Zones 5–10 and needs full sun and a well-drained soil of average fertility. In Zones 5 and 6 sow seeds in early spring indoors, using three or four seeds to a 6-inch pot of commercial potting mix. Transplant the clump of seedlings outdoors without disturbing the roots when night temperatures fall no lower than 55°, setting the clumps 4 inches apart. In Zones 7–10 plant seeds outdoors when warm weather arrives. Do not let the soil become dry in hot, dry periods. Pick the seeds when the seed pods turn brown. Let them dry completely, then rub seed heads to free seeds, and store in an airtight container.

CURDWORT See *Galium*
CURLY PARSLEY See *Petroselinum*

CYNARA
C. cardunculus (cardoon, wild artichoke)

The cardoon, a near relative of the artichoke, is a perennial grown mainly for its edible, celery-like leafstalks though it also has thistle-like blue or purple flowers, ½ to 2 inches across, that bloom in late summer. The pale, ribbed leafstalks may grow up to 5 feet tall and produce thick green leaves with fuzzy white undersides.

HOW TO GROW. Cardoons are hardy in Zones 9 and 10. They can also be grown as annuals in Zones 6–8. They do best in a rich, moist soil and in full sun. Sow seeds in the spring when all danger of frost is past in Zones 9 and 10, or start them in pots indoors in midspring. If you are planting cardoon for eating, sow seeds or set seedlings at the bottom of a 1-foot-deep trench that will later be filled in during the blanching process. Cover seeds with 1 inch of soil, and thin or transplant seedlings to stand about 2 to 3 feet apart. Plants grown for eating are blanched, or whitened, by shielding them from light for a month before harvesting. Tie the stalks together and pile earth around them to the point where the leaves begin. Choose a dry day so the inner leaves are not wet or they will rot. Plants grown as ornamentals should be cut back after flowering in the fall, and protected from frost with a mulch. Or lift the roots and store in a cold frame over the winter for replanting outdoors in spring when all danger of frost is past.

Cardoon may seed itself, or its seeds can be harvested for sowing the following spring. New plants can also be propagated from side shoots that develop when the older plants are cut back for the winter.

D

DAMASK ROSE See *Rosa*
DANDELION See *Taraxacum*
DEAD NETTLE, SPOTTED See *Lamium*

DICTAMNUS
D. albus, also called *D. fraxinella* (gas plant, fraxinella, false dittany, burning bush)

The curious common names of this strange perennial, gas plant and burning bush, come from the fact that in hot, dry, calm weather it produces a vapor that sometimes bursts into flame when ignited; this flash of fire does not hurt the plant. Quirky behavior aside, the gas plant is grown for its lemony

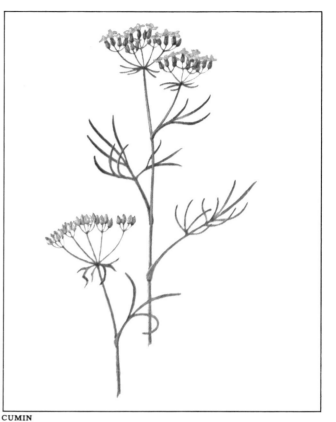

CUMIN
Cuminum cyminum

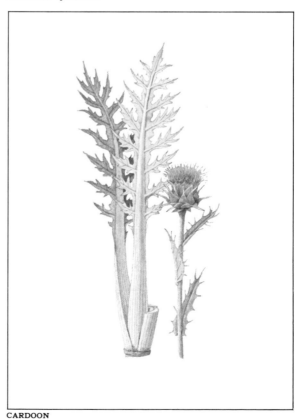

CARDOON
Cynara cardunculus

For climate zones and frost dates, see maps, pages 150–151.

GAS PLANT
Dictamnus albus

FOXGLOVE
Digitalis purpurea

fragrance and its ornamental flowers and seed pods, both of which are popular for indoor flower arrangements.

The gas plant is an erect, bushy herb, 2 feet or more high and wide, with a long life expectancy: in some old gardens there are gas plants more than 50 years old. The plant's shiny, dark green, leathery leaves are composed of oval leaflets arranged in pairs. In early summer, delicate pinkish-purple or white flower spikes flutter 10 to 12 inches above the foliage; the individual flowers are 1 to 2 inches across, and from the base of each blossom project red-purple filaments tipped by green anthers. The flowers do not appear until the plant is three or four years old, but subsequently they grow more abundant each year.

HOW TO GROW. The gas plant, hardy in Zones 3–8, prefers full sun but will tolerate partial shade. It thrives in any well-drained, moderately rich, light-textured soil. Because the gas plant is long lived, dig the soil deeply and add compost or peat moss to prepare for the potentially far-reaching root system. Grow gas plants from nursery stock or propagate them from seed, but if growing them from seed, do not expect blossoms until the third or fourth year. Set the young plants 3 to 4 feet apart in their permanent location. The gas plant requires little care; its foliage dies to the ground each year but the roots send up new growth in the spring.

DIGITALIS
D. purpurea (foxglove, thimbleflower)

Source of a heart stimulant, digitalis, foxglove is a hardy biennial grown in home gardens for its spectacular flower spikes, 4 to 5 feet tall and lined with 1- to 3-inch white, yellow, pink, rose, rusty red or pale purple blossoms, which bloom in the second year. In the first year, the plant forms only a cluster of large, slightly hairy leaves around its base. Foxglove blooms early in the summer, but if the flower stalks are cut back before seeds ripen, it can occasionally be persuaded to bloom again in mid- to late summer.

HOW TO GROW. Foxglove, a European import, has become naturalized and now grows wild in the western United States; it thrives throughout Zones 4–10 except in southern Florida and along the Gulf Coast, where it is grown with difficulty because of the area's humidity. It does best in full sun but will tolerate partial shade, providing color where few plants will flower. It will grow in any well-drained, fertile soil. Start plants from nursery stock or from seeds sown thinly in a carefully prepared seedbed in early summer so that the plants will be well established before frost. When the seedlings are 1 to 2 inches high, transplant them to stand 15 to 18 inches apart. In the fall of the first year, protect the plants with a mulch of pine needles or salt hay, applied after the ground has frozen.

In areas where the soil is not well drained, prevent winter damage by digging up the plants in the fall; leave some soil around the roots and put them in a cold frame. When temperatures drop to freezing, cover them with a 4-inch mulch of straw or salt hay to give them additional protection. In the spring, set the plants out in the garden again as soon as the soil can be worked. Foxglove will reseed itself if seeds are allowed to ripen on the stalk, but to be sure of flowers every year it is best to do your own sowing.

DILL See *Anethum*

DIPSACUS
D. sylvestris (teasel, common teasel)

Teasel is a 5- to 6-foot-tall biennial cultivated for its prickly oval heads, which are used in dried arrangements, and for its seeds, which are an ingredient of bird food. At one time weavers used teasel's comblike heads to raise, or tease, the pile of wool. In the first year the plant produces only a low rosette of coarse, tooth-edged leaves. In the second year prickly stems rise from the rosette, bearing pairs of hairy, lance-shaped leaves, 6 to 20 inches long, covered underneath with bristly spines. During the summer, the stems are capped by flower heads composed of tiny lilac florets that begin to bloom in the center of the head, gradually spreading upward and downward. In late summer, the flower heads turn brown and are filled with dark, rod-shaped seeds.

HOW TO GROW. Common teasel can be cultivated in Zones 3–10. It grows best in full sun but will tolerate partial shade and almost any soil. Sow seeds where plants are to grow in late spring; when seedlings are 2 to 3 inches tall, thin to stand 2 feet apart. If not controlled, teasel spreads by seeding itself and is difficult to eradicate. Cut the flower heads before seeds ripen to keep it in bounds. If you are harvesting teasel for dried arrangements, cut just after seed pods are formed and dry either in an upright position or by hanging in bunches upside down.

DITTANY, FALSE See *Dictamnus*
DITTANY OF CRETE See *Origanum*
DONKEY'S EARS See *Stachys*
DROPWORT See *Filipendula*
DYER'S WEED See *Isatis*

E

EARTH SMOKE See *Fumaria*
EGYPTIAN ONION See *Allium*
ELECAMPANE See *Inula*
ENGLISH LAVENDER See *Lavandula*
ESTRAGON See *Artemisia*

F

FALSE DITTANY See *Dictamnus*
FALSE INDIGO, YELLOW See *Baptisia*
FEATHER GERANIUM See *Chenopodium*
FENNEL See *Foeniculum*
FENNEL, FLORENCE See *Foeniculum*
FENNEL FLOWER See *Nigella*
FENNEL HYSSOP See *Agastache*
FENNEL, SEA See *Crithmum*
FENUGREEK See *Trigonella*

FILIPENDULA
F. hexapetala, also called *F. vulgaris, Spiraea filipendula* (dropwort, meadowsweet)

Sweet-smelling dropwort was the favorite herb of Queen Elizabeth I for masking the odors of unaired rooms. She "did more desire it than any other sweet herb to strew her chambers withal," according to the Elizabethan herbalist John Parkinson. Today this hardy perennial is cultivated as a handsome, lacy addition to a border. The plant grows 15 to 18 inches tall, and has fernlike leaves 6 to 20 inches long in a rosette, from the center of which the flower stems rise. Each stem is capped in early spring with airy clusters of fragrant flowers up to 8 inches across.

HOW TO GROW. Dropwort grows in Zones 4–8 in full sun or light shade and does best in very wet soil, although it will survive in dry soil. Any ordinary garden soil enriched with compost, peat moss or manure is suitable. To start from seeds, plant the seeds in the fall in flats and keep them in a cold frame through the winter. In the spring, set the young plants in the garden, spacing them 12 inches apart; they will

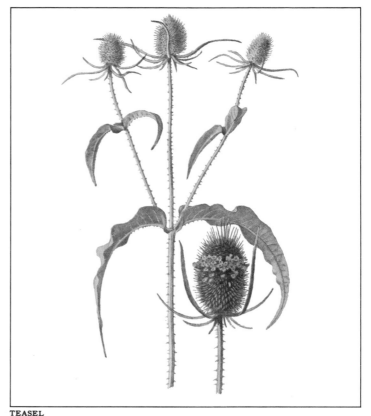

TEASEL
Dipsacus sylvestris

DROPWORT
Filipendula hexapetala

FENNEL
Foeniculum vulgare

FINOCHIO
Foeniculum vulgare dulce

produce foliage the first year and flowers each year thereafter. Dropwort can be left in place indefinitely. In addition to being grown from seed, dropwort can be propagated by dividing root clumps in early spring. The double-flowered form of dropwort, *F. hexapetala flore pleno,* can be increased only by root division.

FINOCHIO See *Foeniculum*
FLORENCE FENNEL See *Foeniculum*
FLORENTINE IRIS See *Iris*
FLORIST'S VIOLET See *Viola*
FOALFOOT See *Tussilago*

FOENICULUM
F. vulgare, also called *F. officinale* (fennel); *F. vulgare dulce* (finochio, Florence fennel)

Fennel, a graceful and bushy plant, is one of the oldest known culinary herbs; its anise-flavored leaves and seeds are highly valued in fish cookery. It is a tender perennial, growing 3 to 4 feet tall, with a thick, glossy main stem and feathery leaves; in summer these are topped by clusters of tiny yellow flowers. By midsummer these clusters begin to droop under the weight of their brown, ribbed seeds, almost ½ inch long, that give off a strong, sweet scent. Each plant yields a total of about ¼ cup of seeds and 1 cup of leaves, in two harvestings per season.

Fennel's smaller cousin finochio, about 2 feet tall, is grown not for its leaves or seeds, but for its bulbous leaf base, which resembles celery. It is a favorite vegetable for salads, especially in Italy.

HOW TO GROW. Fennel, though a tender perennial, is usually grown as an annual in all zones. It does best in full sun, in any garden soil with a pH of 6.0 to 8.0, supplemented by 5-10-5 fertilizer in the amount of 3 ounces to 10 feet of row. Finochio requires the same conditions, but its soil, in addition, should be enriched with compost.

Sow fennel seeds in early spring if you want to harvest seeds as well as leaves. If you grow the plant for its leaves alone, the seeds can be sown continuously at 10-day intervals until summer, assuring a continuous fresh supply. Be sure not to plant fennel and dill close together, since the two cross-pollinate. Fennel can also be propagated by root division in the early spring.

Sow finochio seeds in midsummer; harvest the thick bulbous stem in late fall. Barely cover seeds of both varieties with a thin layer of soil, and when the seedlings are 2 inches high, thin or transplant them to stand about 1 foot apart. Unless it is growing near a fence or a wall, fennel may need to be staked when it gets tall, to protect it from strong winds. Fennel flower heads should be cut before they bloom if the plant is being grown for its leaves alone; this encourages greater leaf growth. Finochio flower heads should also be cut off before they bloom, to encourage the development of a thicker base. When the bulbous base of finochio is about the size of an egg, cover it with soil halfway up, to blanch it. The base will be ready for harvesting in about two weeks.

Fennel leaves can be harvested continuously from the the time the flower heads form until just before the first frost. Use them fresh or dry them in the shade, then store them in an airtight container. Harvest fennel seeds when they ripen, in the fall, and spread them in a thin layer on a screen in the shade to dry, turning them often.

FOX GERANIUM See *Geranium*
FOXGLOVE See *Digitalis*
FRAXINELLA See *Dictamnus*

FRENCH CURLY PARSLEY See *Petroselinum*
FRENCH LAVENDER See *Lavandula*
FRENCH PARSLEY See *Anthriscus*
FRENCH ROSE See *Rosa*
FRENCH SORREL See *Rumex*
FRENCH SPINACH See *Atriplex*
FRENCH TARRAGON See *Artemisia*
FRINGED LAVENDER See *Lavandula*

FUMARIA
F. officinalis (fumitory, earth smoke)

Fumitory is a slender, branching annual that grows about a foot tall. It is sometimes called earth smoke from the hazy, greenish-blue color of its leaves and its delicate shape, which give it the appearance of a cloud of smoke coming out of the ground. It is grown mainly as a soft edging plant; the finely divided leaves weigh down the weak stems. During the summer months, fumitory is topped with clusters of intricately shaped flowers, each about ½ inch long, which resemble the flowers of a snapdragon.

HOW TO GROW. Fumitory grows best in full sun and in light, sandy soil, though it can be grown in any garden that is well drained. Sow the seeds outdoors in the spring, and thin the seedlings so the plants stand 9 inches apart. Fumitory seeds itself readily.

FUMITORY See *Fumaria*

G

GALIUM
G. verum (yellow bedstraw, curdwort, cheese rennet)

Bedstraw is a 1- to 3-foot-tall perennial whose springy stems and leaves, once used to stuff mattresses, give the plant an airy appearance. Mossy leaves, 1 to 2 inches long, circle the stem in groups of six or eight. From spring to late summer, bedstraw blooms in 3- to 4-inch clusters of tiny yellow flowers.

HOW TO GROW. Bedstraw, hardy in Zones 3–6, does well in sun or partial shade and will grow in almost any soil. Favored for rock gardens, bedstraw sprawls naturally, but can be staked if upright growth is desired. It will seed itself, but is most easily propagated from root clumps planted early in the spring, 1 foot apart. Every two or three years, divide the root clumps in the spring.

GARDEN CRESS See *Lepidium*
GARDEN HELIOTROPE See *Valeriana*
GARDEN SAGE See *Salvia*
GARDEN THYME See *Thymus*
GARLIC See *Allium*
GAS PLANT See *Dictamnus*

GERANIUM
G. robertianum (herb Robert, fox geranium, bloodwort)

Herb Robert is a very old wild member of the true geranium genus (plants commonly called geraniums are of the *Pelargonium* genus). It is an annual whose natural habitat is rocky woods. Though its stems grow about 15 inches long, herb Robert sprawls so much that it appears to be nearly prostrate. Its thick central stem, reddish and hairy, branches into deeply lobed leaves, 2 to 3 inches across, which have a strong, unpleasant odor. All summer long ½-inch flowers bloom in pairs continuously. The seed pods that follow burst open when ripe with surprising force, making the plant's reproductive mechanism difficult to control.

HOW TO GROW. Herb Robert grows in Zones 2–6. It does

FUMITORY
Fumaria officinalis

YELLOW BEDSTRAW
Galium verum

HERB ROBERT
Geranium robertianum

For climate zones and frost dates, see maps, pages 150–151.

COMMON HELIOTROPE
Heliotropium peruvianum

HYSSOP
Hyssopus officinalis

best in an environment that simulates its natural habitat—a shady spot with moist, well-drained soil. It is raised from seed sown in the early fall.

GERANIUM, CLORINDA See *Pelargonium*
GERANIUM, FEATHER See *Chenopodium*
GERANIUM, SCENTED See *Pelargonium*
GERMAN CHAMOMILE See *Matricaria*
GERMAN IRIS See *Iris*
GERMANDER See *Teucrium*
GIANT CHERVIL See *Myrrhis*
GOOD-KING-HENRY See *Chenopodium*
GREAT MULLEIN See *Verbascum*
GREEK HAY SEED See *Trigonella*

H

HEART'S EASE See *Viola*
HELIOTROPE, GARDEN See *Valeriana*

HELIOTROPIUM
H. peruvianum, also called *H. arborescens* (common heliotrope, cherry pie)

Common heliotrope, a tender perennial shrub that used to provide a popular toilet-water scent, is usually treated now as an annual for flower beds and window boxes. It normally grows as a bush 6 to 12 inches tall, but by trimming off the shoots along the central stem you can train it into a tree form. Its tiny ⅛- to ¼-inch flowers have an appealing vanilla scent; they bloom densely in 2- to 4-inch clusters from spring to early fall. The oblong pointed leaves, 1 to 3 inches long, are wrinkled and hairy, with prominent veins.

HOW TO GROW. Common heliotrope grows in Zones 3–10 as a garden annual and in Zones 9 and 10 on the West Coast as a perennial. It can be treated as a perennial in any zone if it is planted in a pot and taken indoors during the winter. It does well in any garden soil in either full sun or light shade, but the soil should be kept moist. To grow it from seeds, sow the seeds ½ inch apart in pots about seven to nine weeks before night temperatures can be expected to stay above 55°. Transfer the seedlings to the open ground when night temperatures are consistently mild, setting the plants 12 inches apart. Common heliotrope can also be propagated from stem cuttings (choose young flowerless side shoots taken in the fall and kept indoors over the winter). Grown indoors, common heliotrope needs at least four hours of direct sunlight a day. Keep the soil moist but not soggy and fertilize the plant at two-week intervals with a liquid house-plant fertilizer used at half strength.

HEN-AND-CHICKENS See *Sempervivum*
HERB OF GRACE See *Ruta*
HERB ROBERT See *Geranium*
HOLY THISTLE See *Silybum*
HOP MARJORAM See *Origanum*
HOREHOUND See *Marrubium*
HORSERADISH See *Armoracia*
HOUSELEEK See *Sempervivum*

HYSSOPUS
H. officinalis (hyssop)

Once popular as a household strewing herb, fragrant when walked upon, and as a flavoring for gamy meats, hyssop is valued today for its decorative qualities. It is a shrublike semievergreen perennial, 18 to 24 inches tall, that is often used as a low hedge. Throughout the summer, clusters of tiny blossoms of blue, pink or white grow in whorls around the plant's flower spikes. Scented hyssop blossoms attract bees and butterflies.

HOW TO GROW. Hyssop grows in Zones 3–7 in sun or partial shade, and will thrive in any well-drained soil. Sow seeds ¼ inch deep in spring or fall and thin seedlings to stand 1 foot apart; for faster results start with nursery stock. Hyssop is very hardy and its roots do not need winter protection, but the stems should be cut back to the ground each fall or spring to encourage new growth. After three or four years plants grow woody and produce less foliage; to renew a sparse hedge divide the roots of mature plants in the spring or fall or start new plants from seeds.

I

INDIAN CRESS See *Tropaeolum*
INDIGO, WILD or YELLOW FALSE See *Baptisia*

INULA

I. helenium (elecampane, horseheal)

Elecampane is grown in some regions for its bitter, aromatic root, which is used as a flavoring in liqueurs and cordials, but its bright yellow flowers, resembling miniature sunflowers, make it a handsome background plant for the garden. It is a hardy perennial, 4 to 6 feet tall, with coarse, deeply veined leaves, downy on the underside; leaves at the base of the plant may be as much as 20 inches long and 8 inches wide. The flowers are 3 to 4 inches across and bloom in mid- to late summer.

HOW TO GROW. Native to Europe, elecampane grows wild from Nova Scotia and Ontario to North Carolina and Missouri, and is hardy in Zones 3–8. It will grow in full sun or partial shade and thrives in almost any moist soil. Sow seeds outdoors in the spring or fall. When plants are 2 to 3 inches tall, thin or transplant them to stand 2 to 4 feet apart. Elecampane can also be propagated from root divisions in the spring or fall. Every three years the plants should be renewed by dividing their roots.

ELECAMPANE
Inula helenium

IRIS

I. germanica florentina (orris, German iris, Florentine iris)

Orris is a kind of iris grown for its violet-scented root, which is used in dried and powdered form as a fixative to reinforce other fragrances. An ingredient in many perfumes, it can be added to sachets and potpourris, but it must be used with caution, since some people are allergic to it. Its flower inspired the fleur-de-lis of French heraldry.

The stiff, sword-shaped leaves grow 1½ to 2 feet high. Large white flowers with lavender veins and yellow beards bloom very early in spring.

HOW TO GROW. Orris grows well through Zones 3–10 except in the warm, moist climate of Florida and the Gulf Coast. A perennial, it needs full sun and will grow in any well-drained soil. It is grown from rhizomes planted any time the soil can be worked, but preferably in early summer. Place the rhizomes horizontally so that their tops lie just at the surface of the soil, 1 to 1½ feet apart, with the stubby anchoring roots pointing downward. The plants will produce foliage that will die down in the fall; flowers will appear the following spring. When they finish flowering, cut back the flower stalks to discourage seed production. Orris roots multiply rapidly, and can be dug up, divided and transplanted or harvested every three or four years in early summer immediately after flowering.

Harvest orris roots by digging, washing and peeling them; then put them in the sun to dry. Store the roots in a dry place for one or two years to develop their characteristic

ORRIS
Iris germanica florentina

For climate zones and frost dates, see maps, pages 150–151.

WOAD
Isatis tinctoria

JASMINE
Jasminum officinale

violet fragrance. After this storage period, they are ready to be ground into powder.

ISATIS

I. tinctoria (woad, dyer's-weed)

Woad is a yellow-flowered member of the mustard family, once famous for the blue dye extracted from its leaves. Today, both the flower panicles and the pendulous seeds are popular for fresh flower arrangements. It is a biennial, forming a low rosette of oval leaves in the first year of growth. The following spring, sturdy stems rise 1½ to 4 feet tall bearing lance-shaped leaves, which graduate from a maximum of about 4 inches long at the base to 1½ inches at the top; the leaves have the blue-green color of broccoli leaves. Woad blooms in early summer in panicles that spread as much as 2 feet wide. The flowers are followed by black seeds that hang from the stems for several weeks.

HOW TO GROW. Woad is hardy in Zones 3–10 and grows in partial shade or full sun, in any rich, well-drained garden soil. Sow seeds in the late summer so the plants will be well established before winter. Thin or transplant seedlings, when they are 2 to 3 inches high, spacing them 6 to 12 inches apart. Seedlings are best transplanted in the early spring when the ground is moist. If the seed heads of the plant are cut before ripening, woad acts as a short-lived perennial but if it is allowed to blossom normally, it will reseed itself.

ITALIAN PLAIN-LEAVED PARSLEY See *Petroselinum*

J

JACOB'S STAFF See *Verbascum*

JASMINUM

J. officinale (jasmine, common jasmine, white jasmine, tea jasmine)

The fragrance of jasmine on a summer night has inspired poets to verse and its petals are a mainstay of the perfume industry. In its native Kashmir it is a semievergreen vine climbing to a height of 30 or 40 feet; in southern gardens, greenhouses and homes it is generally kept pruned to a more manageable size and is treated as a shrub. Jasmine leaves grow in pairs, with each leaf made up of three to seven leaflets that range in size from ½ to 2½ inches long; the snow-white, sweetly scented flowers bloom in clusters at the ends of new growth the whole summer.

HOW TO GROW. Jasmine grows outdoors only in Zones 7–10. It does well in full sun or partial shade in any garden soil. In areas where it can be grown outdoors, plant nursery stock in either spring or fall. Prune only after flowering, since the flowers appear on young branches. Propagate additional plants from 3- to 6-inch stem cuttings taken from new growth in early spring, rooting them in moist sand.

Jasmine does well as a house plant, and unlike most summer-flowering plants, often continues to bloom indoors all winter long. It thrives on high humidity, night temperatures of 50° to 55°, day temperatures above 65°, and a rich potting soil. It requires at least four hours of direct sunlight daily. During periods of active growth, feed indoor plants an all-purpose liquid fertilizer biweekly, mixed at half strength. Do not feed during rest periods. Set pots on trays of moist pebbles indoors to supply extra humidity. Keep the soil barely damp in the winter, but water generously from March to October, keeping the soil moist but not soggy. Indoor plants may need drastic pruning; cut back wandering branches after they have flowered. The average size of indoor plants is 2 to 3 feet, but they can grow 5 or 6 feet tall.

JERUSALEM OAK See *Chenopodium*
JOHNNY-JUMP-UP See *Viola*

K

KNITBONE See *Symphytum*
KNOTTED MARJORAM See *Origanum*

L

LADY'S MANTLE See *Alchemilla*
LAMB MINT See *Mentha*
LAMB'S EARS See *Stachys*

LAMIUM

L. maculatum (spotted dead nettle, cobbler's bench)

This wandering perennial member of the mint family looks like a stinging nettle but does not sting, hence its name dead nettle. The stem is hollow and either erect or ascending from a sprawling base to a height of 6 inches to 2 feet, depending upon soil fertility and moisture. During the summer, the plant produces 1- to 2-inch terminal clusters of curious hooded blossoms about 1 inch long, white or magenta in color. Bees are much attracted to dead nettle, which is grown today as a decorative ground cover.

HOW TO GROW. Dead nettle grows in Zones 3–8; it does best in partial shade and moist soil, but will tolerate sun. Almost any soil will suit it. A European import, it now grows wild in most of eastern Canada and the United States. Sow seeds or start plants from root divisions in the spring. Space plants 1 foot apart. Dead nettle needs little care.

LAURUS

L. nobilis (sweet bay, bay, laurel, bay leaf)

Sweet bay is an aromatic evergreen whose fragrant leaves, 1 to 3 inches long, are used for seasoning and are a standard ingredient of the *bouquet garni* of French cooking. In its native Mediterranean soil, sweet bay grows into a towering tree, 40 to 60 feet high, but in the United States it is usually a shrub, 3 to 10 feet tall, grown in a large tub or pot. The shrub can be sheared into almost any shape, hence it is a favorite for topiary sculpture. Although sweet bay rarely blooms in northern climates, in semitropical regions it produces tiny yellow blossoms in spring at the intersection of the leaves and the stem, followed by purple-black berries.

HOW TO GROW. Except in the mild climate of Zones 8–10, where it grows well outdoors all year round, sweet bay is usually kept in a tub or pot so it can be moved indoors in the winter. Outdoors, it needs to be shaded from the heat of summer sun and protected from the wind. Inside, it does best in a greenhouse with a controlled temperature between 38° and 45°. It can also be grown as a house plant in room temperatures ranging between 40° and 65°, if it gets at least four hours of direct sunlight or bright reflected light a day, or 12 hours of strong artificial light.

Start sweet bay from nursery stock planted in commercial potting soil; cuttings require more than a year to root and even then do not always take. Keep the soil moist in spring and moderately dry the rest of the year; good drainage is essential. Do not feed for at least three months after planting. Then, feed twice a year, in early spring and in early summer, with any house-plant fertilizer.

Sweet bay leaves can be used fresh or dried, and can be harvested at any time of the year. To dry the leaves, hang sprigs in a warm dark room where the temperature does not exceed 70°. When they are partly dry but not brittle, spread the leaves on a flat surface, cover them with a clean cloth and weight them with a board for about 10 days to flatten

SPOTTED DEAD NETTLE
Lamium maculatum

SWEET BAY
Laurus nobilis

For climate zones and frost dates, see maps, pages 150–151.

FRINGED LAVENDER
Lavandula dentata

them. Store the flattened leaves in an airtight container. Caution: Do not confuse this laurel with mountain laurel, a native of the United States, which has poisonous leaves.

LAVANDULA
L. dentata (fringed lavender); *L. officinalis,* also called *L. vera* and *L. spica* (English lavender, true lavender); *L. stoechas* (French or Spanish lavender)

The long-lasting fragrant leaves and blossoms of lavender have been used for centuries in dried sachets, scented soaps, perfumes and aromatic tobaccos. Lavender salts long have been used as a stimulant to prevent fainting. In the garden, lavender makes a sweet-smelling border plant along pathways or among rocks.

All of the lavenders are bushy perennials growing 1 to 3 feet tall, and all bear spikes of ¼- to ½-inch flowers, usually arranged in multiple whorls of six to 10 blossoms around each stem. Both the flowers and the foliage of all three plants have a sweet aroma, but the colors and configurations are somewhat different. Fringed lavender's 1- to 1½-inch dark green foliage is fernlike, with deeply indented edges. Spanish lavender and English lavender have ½- to 2-inch-long, needle-like foliage but English lavender's leaves are blue-green, while those of French lavender have a gray cast. The lavenders bloom in midsummer, the English bearing gray-blue flowers, the fringed, blue flowers and the Spanish, deep purple or white flowers.

HOW TO GROW. English lavender is hardy in Zones 5–10 although it requires a mulch in Zones 5 and 6 to protect it from winter cold. The more delicate Spanish lavender is hardy in Zones 8–10, and fringed lavender is hardy only in Zones 9 and 10. Both must be taken indoors for the winter wherever temperatures are likely to fall below freezing. They flourish in direct sunlight and dry, sandy, well-drained alkaline soil; infertile soil seems to improve the fragrance. Because lavender seeds take about six weeks to germinate and seedlings grow very slowly, the plants are usually propagated from stem cuttings, which can be taken at any time of year. Plant rooted cuttings in the garden in spring, in soil supplemented with ground limestone to neutralize acidity. Space plants 2 to 3 feet apart. In the first year of growth nip off the flower spikes before they bloom in order to make bushes more compact. Any old woody growth should be pruned away every year in the spring. Established plants can be left undisturbed indefinitely.

Harvest lavender flowers after the plant's second year; harvest the leaves at any time. To harvest flowers, cut the stems just as buds start to open, when their color and fragrance are greatest. Hang them in bunches, upside down, or dry them flat on a tray in a warm, airy, shady place for several weeks until they become crisp. Strip off the dried leaves and flowers from the stems and store them in a container that is airtight.

Spanish and fringed lavender can be grown indoors as pot plants. They require a minimum of five hours of direct sunlight a day. Use a commercial potting soil supplemented with ground limestone. Feed with any house plant fertilizer, mixed at half strength and applied half as often as the package suggests. Water until the soil is barely moist, and let the soil become dry between waterings. Indoor-grown lavender needs good air circulation around it to keep the leaves from blackening. As a pot plant, lavender usually grows only 1 to 2 feet tall.

LAVENDER COTTON See *Santolina*
LEEK See *Allium*

ENGLISH LAVENDER
Lavandula officinalis

FRENCH LAVENDER
Lavandula stoechas

LEMON BALM See *Melissa*
LEMON-SCENTED GERANIUM See *Pelargonium*
LEMON THYME See *Thymus*
LEMON VERBENA See *Lippia*

LEPIDIUM

L. sativum (garden cress, pepper cress)

Garden cress, an annual that grows 18 inches tall, bears leaves that can be eaten in a salad. But most often garden cress is harvested for eating soon after germination, before the first true leaves develop. Then it is used as a peppery garnish for soups and sandwiches in combination with the similar seed leaves of mustard.

HOW TO GROW. Garden cress flourishes outdoors in Zones 3–10 in sun or light shade and a fertile, well-drained soil; seeds can be sown in the garden at intervals from very early spring through the summer to provide young leaves. At any time of the year, sow seeds thickly and evenly in shallow pots or other containers filled with potting soil. Press the soil flat and water it, then place in bright light at a temperature of 65° to 70°. In 10 to 12 days, seedlings will be ready for harvesting with a scissors. If you grow cress and mustard together in the same container, sow the cress seed first and the mustard four days later, because mustard germinates more quickly than cress.

LEVISTICUM

L. officinale (lovage)

Lovage is a giant among herbs, a kitchen-garden plant that, at maturity, reaches a height of 3 to 7 feet, but it acquires this size over a period of about four years, dying back to the ground each winter. It is a perennial that somewhat resembles celery in appearance, taste and use. The dark green leaves are used as a salad green or to flavor soups and stews; the seeds add a celery-like flavor to many dishes. During colonial times, lovage's thick roots were candied as a tasty confection.

Lovage blooms in midsummer, producing umbrella-shaped clusters of small yellow-green flowers, 3 inches across, which are allowed to ripen for their seeds. Lovage does not mature until its second year, at which point a single plant will produce ½ cup of seeds, 4 cups of leaves and six to eight stalks.

HOW TO GROW. Lovage can be grown throughout the United States but with difficulty in southern Florida and along the Gulf Coast because it needs cold weather to complete its growth cycle. It adapts to full sun or partial shade, and does best in a rich, moist soil of pH 6.0 to 7.0 supplemented with compost or manure. It can be started from seeds or root divisions; for best results the seeds must be planted as soon as they are ripe, but in any case must be less than three years old to germinate. Sow seeds outdoors in early fall, covering them with about ¼ inch of soil, or sow seeds indoors in 3- to 4-inch peat pots in early spring. When night temperatures remain above 40° in the spring, set the plants in the garden, placing them about 3 feet apart. You can also start lovage from root divisions in the spring. Fertilize every spring with a handful of 5-10-5 fertilizer scratched in around the base of each plant.

If lovage is raised for its leaves, do not let it flower. Leaves can generally be cut three times during the season; cut only the outside leaves, not the tender heart. To preserve leaves for winter use, dry them on their stems by hanging them in a cool dark place; store in an airtight container. Seed heads intended for flavoring should be dried flat under the same conditions of light and temperature as described for drying leaves, and stored in the same manner.

GARDEN CRESS
Lepidium sativum

LOVAGE
Levisticum officinale

For climate zones and frost dates, see maps, pages 150–151.

LEMON VERBENA
Lippia citriodora

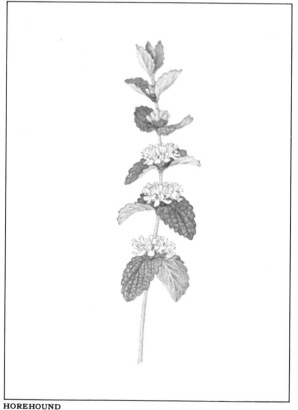

HOREHOUND
Marrubium vulgare

LIPPIA

L. citriodora, also called *Aloysia triphylla*, *A. citriodora* and *Verbena triphylla* (lemon verbena)

Lemon verbena is an aromatic semievergreen shrub whose lemon-scented leaves are used to flavor foods, fruit drinks and teas, and to perfume colognes and potpourri. Usually grown in tubs, this plant can be pruned to any height although in its native Chile it grows 6 to 10 feet tall. Outdoors in Zones 9 and 10, or when grown indoors, it remains green the year round; in Zones 7 and 8, the narrow 2- to 4-inch leaves fall off during the winter and the plant appears dead until new growth appears the following spring. Tiny, barely perceptible mauve and white flowers bloom infrequently on slender panicles during the summer and fall.

HOW TO GROW. From Zone 7 south, plant lemon verbena in the open ground in any light, well-drained soil in full sun, spacing shrubs about 2 feet apart. North of Zone 7, plant it in pots to be placed outdoors in summer and brought indoors in winter before the first frost. Pot-grown plants thrive on a mixture of equal parts of loam, sand and leaf mold, and do best with night temperatures of 50° to 55°, rising to 70° to 75° in daytime. They require at least five or six hours of direct sunlight a day. To promote new growth, cut back the stalks of potted plants in February to within 6 inches of the soil, and for the same reason repot plants in a fresh soil mixture every two or three years. It is even better to discard old plants after two years, replacing them with young ones. To propagate, root cuttings of new growth taken in the spring. Lemon verbena is vulnerable to red spiders and plants should be sprayed frequently and forcefully with plain water to control these pests.

To harvest lemon verbena, pick the leaves at any time and dry them rapidly in a warm dark place. Stored in an airtight container, they will retain their fragrance for years.

LOVAGE See *Levisticum*
LOVE-IN-A-MIST See *Nigella*

M

MARIGOLD, POT See *Calendula*
MARJORAM or KNOTTED MARJORAM See *Origanum*

MARRUBIUM

M. vulgare (horehound)

Musky, rather bitter-tasting horehound—taken in the form of syrup, candy, tea and even snuff—was once the sovereign remedy for coughs. It is a hardy perennial, 2 to 3 feet high, with velvety leaves 1 to 2 inches long and down-covered stems. From July through September, tiny white blossoms encircle the stems at intervals, providing bees with nectar for a tasty honey. Because the seeds have hooklike appendages that fasten onto animals, the seeds spread far afield, causing horehound to be regarded as a weed in some places.

HOW TO GROW. Horehound needs full sun and grows easily in any poor, dry soil. It grows in Zones 3–10. Horehound may be started from seeds sown in the spring or fall; cover the seeds with ½ inch of soil. Horehound seedlings germinate erratically, and one may appear long before others. When the seedlings are 4 to 5 inches high, thin them to stand 8 to 10 inches apart; this relatively close spacing will help keep the stems erect. Horehound needs little care except weeding.

MARSH MALLOW See *Althaea*

MATRICARIA

M. chamomilla (German chamomile)

German chamomile is often confused with Roman chamomile (see *Anthemis*). Both are used for herbal teas, and they share a common name, an apple-like fragrance and daisy-like flowers. But the two plants are not botanically related. German chamomile grows 6 to 18 inches high, erect rather than creeping, and it is an annual rather than a perennial. The yellow centers of its ¾-inch white flowers are domed and hollow on the inside, and bloom at the ends of slender stems from spring to fall. The deeply cut, shiny green leaves give the plant a feathery appearance.

HOW TO GROW. German chamomile can be grown in Zones 3–10. It needs full sun and will grow in any light, dry soil. Sow seeds in the late summer or early spring, or start them indoors in flats or pots in late winter. Sprinkle them on top of the soil; do not cover—they are very fine—and keep the soil moist but not soggy during the germination period. Thin or transplant the seedlings to stand 8 to 12 inches apart.

Harvest chamomile when the flowers are in full bloom and on a sunny day. Spread the flower heads thinly on a clean cloth and dry them in the sun. Then remove and discard any leaves or pieces of stem; store the flowers in an airtight container in a cool dry place.

MEADOWSWEET See *Filipendula*

MELISSA

M. officinalis (balm, lemon balm, sweet balm)

Often confused with lemon thyme and lemon verbena, lemon balm is a mintlike, fast-spreading perennial, 1 to 2 feet tall and equally wide, grown for its multipurpose lemon-scented leaves, which are used as a seasoning for veal or poultry, floated on cold drinks, brewed in teas and used in perfumes. Lemon balm's leaves are 1 to 3 inches long, and from early summer into fall the plant produces small clusters of inconspicuous creamy-white flowers rich in nectar.

HOW TO GROW. Lemon balm is grown in Zones 4–10, though with some difficulty in southern Florida and along the Gulf Coast because it needs cold weather to complete its annual growth cycle. It does best in full sun or light shade and a light, dry, relatively poor soil with a pH of 6.0 to 8.0. Like other lemon-scented herbs, it produces more intense flavor and aroma under infertile growing conditions. Seeds germinate slowly and should be sown indoors eight to 10 weeks before the expected date of the last frost for transplanting outdoors when all danger of frost is past; or better still, sow seeds outdoors in late fall to germinate the following spring. Do not cover the seeds with soil; they are very tiny. When seedlings are about 2 inches high, thin or transplant them to stand 18 inches apart. You also can start plants from root divisions in early spring, when the new leaves first appear, or from stem cuttings taken in spring or summer.

Fresh leaves of lemon balm can be picked for use at any time. To harvest leaves for drying, cut just before or after flowering and spread on a tray or screen in the shade. To retain color and flavor, dry as quickly as possible, preferably at temperatures above 90°. Store dried leaves in an airtight container. A mature plant produces 2 cups of fresh leaves when it is first harvested, and two slightly less bountiful harvests later in the season.

Lemon balm grown indoors requires at least five hours of direct sunlight a day or 14 to 16 hours of artificial light. Start plants from seed at any time, or bring plants in from the garden in late summer. Lemon balm grown indoors should be pruned periodically to produce a bushy plant 6 to 8 inches high; leaves for flavoring can be picked when the plant reaches a height of 6 inches.

GERMAN CHAMOMILE
Matricaria chamomilla

BALM
Melissa officinalis

For climate zones and frost dates, see maps, pages 150–151.

PEPPERMINT
Mentha piperita officinalis

PENNYROYAL
Mentha pulegium

MENTHA

M. piperita officinalis (peppermint); *M. pulegium* (penny-royal, pudding grass); *M. rotundifolia* (apple mint, round-leaved mint, woolly mint); *M. spicata* (spearmint, lamb mint)

The mints are a large and popular family of herbs, cultivated for their intensely flavored, cool-tasting leaves. They grow easily and spread rapidly through wandering, deep-reaching roots which, if not contained, quickly invade parts of the garden where they are not wanted. The mints listed here are perennials. Their stems are between 1 and 3 feet tall and bear pairs of opposing tooth-edged leaves. Their tiny flowers bloom in clusters in terminal spikes and are usually followed by round brown seeds.

Peppermint can be identified by its fragrant leaves, which grow on short stalks, and by its stems, which have a reddish cast. Its dense spikes of violet flowers bloom in late summer, but since peppermint comes from crosses with other mints, it is sterile and the flowers rarely go to seed. Consequently, it can be propagated only by stem cuttings or root divisions.

Pennyroyal, a bitter-tasting mint whose unusual flavor is no longer popular, makes an aromatic ground cover. In former times, it was used as a flavoring for puddings and sauces, hence its name pudding grass. The plant's creeping stems, 18 to 24 inches long, have ½-inch oval leaves covered with tiny hairs. In midsummer, lavender-blue or pink flowers rise in tiers on 6- to 12-inch flower spikes above the otherwise prostrate plant.

Apple mint is sometimes called round-leaved mint for its 1- to 4-inch rounded leaves that have wrinkled surfaces covered with a dense whitish down. This fruity-tasting mint grows ½ to 3 feet tall and in midsummer bears 2- to 4-inch branching spikes of grayish-white blossoms that deepen to pink or violet. Apple mint is less popular as a culinary herb than other mints because of its hairy foliage, but the flowers and leaves are often cut for fresh flower arrangements. One variety of apple mint, called pineapple mint *(M. rotundifolia variegata),* has foliage streaked with light yellow or white and grows only 10 inches tall.

Spearmint, the classic ingredient in mint juleps, is the most strongly flavored of the mints. Its leaves can be floated in drinks, candied for sauces and jellies, sprinkled on meats, or eaten fresh in salads and with vegetables. Its erect stems grow 1 to 2 feet tall, and its leaves, practically hairless and deeply veined, are about 2 inches long. In midsummer dense flower spikes of violet or pink blossoms rise above the green foliage on a central stem.

A mature mint plant produces about 2 cups of leaves at the first cutting and will yield somewhat smaller amounts at 10-day intervals thereafter.

HOW TO GROW. All the mints except pennyroyal are hardy throughout the United States, although they are cultivated with some difficulty in the mild, moist climate of southern Florida and along the Gulf Coast. Pennyroyal is not hardy where winter temperatures fall below 5° and needs to be moved indoors. The mints grow well in direct sunlight or partial shade and do best in rich, fairly moist soil with a pH of 5.5 to 6.5, supplemented with compost. Apple mint, sometimes called "dryland" mint, will grow in less moist soil.

To prevent mint from taking over the garden, choose a restricted position, or block the wandering roots with underground barriers of metal or plastic strips 6 to 10 inches deep. Mint can also be planted in flowerpots or open-ended barrels, sunk into the earth. Dig compost deep into the soil to enrich it, but do not use manure; the latter carries a disfiguring mint rust fungus. Mints are usually started in the spring or fall from root divisions set 12 to 15 inches apart, or from stem cuttings. To increase the plant's leaf production, nip off flower spikes before they open. Where winter temperatures remain below 0° for extended periods, protect plants with a mulch of salt hay or pine needles. Each spring, chop matted mint roots with a sharp spade 3 or 4 inches deep. Sprinkle compost or a dusting of 5-10-5 fertilizer over the ground at this time. Renew mints every three years by dividing and resetting the roots in the spring or fall; at this time peppermint, which does not do well in the same place for more than a few years, should be transferred to a new location.

Mint leaves can be picked for use fresh at any time. To harvest the leaves for drying, cut the stems down to the first two sets of leaves just before the flowers open. Hang upside down to dry in a warm, dark, well-ventilated place. Pick the dried leaves from the stems and rub them between the palms of the hands to crush them slightly; then store them in an airtight container.

All mints can be grown indoors but apple mint makes the most handsome, compact plant; the other varieties tend to become scrawny. Indoor mints require at least five hours of strong, direct sunlight a day. Pot in the spring or early fall in containers that provide room for the creeping roots. Use a commercial potting soil. Cut back stems frequently to 4 to 6 inches for better-tasting leaves and to keep the plants from flowering. Keep soil moist but not soggy, and feed with a liquid house-plant fertilizer, used half strength, every three to four weeks. If plants start to yellow, repot them in a larger container or divide the mass of roots into small sections and repot into separate pots.

MILFOIL See *Achillea*
MILK THISTLE See *Silybum*

MONARDA
M. didyma (bee balm, bergamot, Oswego tea)

Bergamot is a striking member of the mint family that stands 3 feet tall on an erect stem and produces shaggy flaming-red flowers, 2 to 3 inches across, made up of numerous trumpet-shaped florets. These aromatic flowers bloom throughout the summer and are a great favorite with hummingbirds and bees. They make fine cut flowers. Bergamot is native to the United States and its citrus-flavored leaves, 4 to 6 inches long, were used as a tea by the Oswego Indians of upstate New York. Oswego tea was also drunk by the rebellious colonial patriots who were boycotting British tea. Today bergamot leaves are most often used as flavoring for fruit cups and preserves.

HOW TO GROW. Bergamot grows in Zones 4–10 except in Florida and along the Gulf Coast, where the warm humid winters hinder its annual growth cycle. It does best in full sun but tolerates light shade, and will thrive in any moist soil that is rich in organic matter such as manure, compost or leaf mold. When grown from seed, it takes more than a year to become established, so it is usually started from nursery stock or root divisions. The latter are easy to take, for bergamot's roots are shallow and far ranging. Dig up the root clump in the early spring, discard the inner, older portion, and set the divisions 12 to 15 inches apart. To increase the strength of seedling-grown plants in later years, cut off the flower heads the first year before they bloom. Thereafter, cutting flowers right after they bloom often stimulates a second flowering in the same year. Weed bergamot by hand to avoid damaging the shallow roots. In the fall, prune plants to within an inch of the ground. Every three or four years, bergamot clumps should be divided to prevent overcrowding.

Bergamot leaves can be harvested either just before or just

APPLE MINT
Mentha rotundifolia

SPEARMINT
Mentha spicata

BEE BALM
Monarda didyma

SWEET CICELY
Myrrhis odorata

MYRTLE
Myrtus communis

after the plant flowers. To dry the leaves, strip them from the stalk and dry in the shade on a screen or tray for two or three days; then store in an airtight container.

MOTHER-OF-THYME See *Thymus*
MULLEIN, GREAT See *Verbascum*
MUSTARD See *Brassica*

MYRRHIS

M. odorata (sweet cicely, giant chervil, anise fern)

Sweet cicely, described as "that herbe of very good and pleasant smell" by the 16th Century herbalist Gerard, is a graceful 2- to 3-foot-high perennial whose every part—seeds, roots, leaves and blossoms—is pervaded by a sweet anise-like taste and fragrance; for this reason it is sometimes called the candy plant. The taproot can be cooked and eaten as a vegetable, and the oil can be extracted from its seeds to be used as a flavoring in liqueurs, but it is grown in gardens mainly for its handsome foliage, which is downy on the underside. In the late spring, the plant's tall hollow stems bear 2- to 4-inch clusters of white flowers that are attractive to bees; the flowers are followed by crowns of shiny, brownish-black seeds, ¾ to 1 inch long.

HOW TO GROW. Sweet cicely is grown in Zones 4–10, although with some difficulty in southern Florida and along the Gulf Coast because it needs cold weather to complete its annual growth cycle. It needs partial shade and a moist acid soil of pH 5.5 to 6.5, supplemented with compost or manure. Dig the bed deep, to accommodate the plant's deep taproot, and plant the seeds in the late summer or early fall, covering them with ¼ inch of soil; sweet cicely seeds germinate best after freezing during the winter months. In the spring, when the seedlings are about 2 inches tall, thin them to stand 2 feet apart. If seeds are allowed to dry and fall from the plant, sweet cicely will seed itself. It can also be propagated from upper sections of the taproot; make sure, however, that each section contains an eye.

Leaves can be harvested for use fresh from the time they unfold in spring until late fall. Seeds may be harvested when they are ripe, but many gardeners prefer to pick green, immature seeds in midsummer to flavor herb mixtures and salads. A mature plant will produce about 4 cups of leaves and ½ cup of seeds each season.

MYRTUS

M. communis (myrtle)

One of several plants used by the ancient Greeks to make crowns for poets and athletes, this species of myrtle is a dense evergreen shrub. Under ideal conditions it grows to a height of 10 to 15 feet, but most garden plants grow 3 to 8 feet tall, depending on the variety. Plants grown in pots are usually only 8 to 12 inches tall. Every part of the myrtle—leaves, flowers, berries and bark—is aromatic. The shiny leaves, 1 to 2 inches long, give off a particularly strong and pleasant scent when crushed. The sweet-smelling flowers, ¾ inch across, bloom from late spring to midsummer. They are followed by ½-inch berries, which the Athenians dried and used as a condiment, like pepper. Myrtle also provides an excellent hedge.

HOW TO GROW. Myrtle grows outdoors in Zones 9 and 10. Elsewhere it should be grown in pots or tubs and moved indoors during the winter. It will grow in sun or light shade in almost any well-drained garden soil, but it does not tolerate wet soil. Myrtle is easily propagated from cuttings of half-ripened shoots taken in midsummer; it can also be grown from seeds or by layering.

When it is grown as a hedge, myrtle should be pruned in the spring, before new growth starts. It can be easily trained to any desired shape and size. Myrtle grown indoors tolerates low light conditions; even reflected light near a window is adequate.

N

NASTURTIUM See *Tropaeolum*

NASTURTIUM

N. officinale, also called *Roripa nasturtium-aquaticum, Radicula nasturtium-quaticum* and *Sisymbrium nasturtium-aquaticum* (watercress)

Peppery-tasting watercress is a semiaquatic, creeping perennial whose leaves are popular in salads and as a garnish for meat. The many-branched plant grows in shallow water, either submerged or floating, its stems stretching 2 feet or more in length. Each dark green compound leaf consists of three to 11 leaflets, ½ to ¾ inch across, growing off a slightly paler stem that is usually submerged; each group of leaflets is between 5 and 6 inches long. Watercress keeps sending out new roots and a single plant will grow indefinitely until freezing weather. During the early summer, small, white four-petaled flowers bloom in loose clusters at the extreme ends of the stems.

HOW TO GROW. Watercress can be grown throughout Zones 3–10 and is a commercial crop in Alabama, California and Virginia. It may be found growing wild in streams throughout the United States. It grows best in shallow, slowly moving water, particularly cool streams, although it will adapt to improvised irrigation trenches and can also be grown, with less vigor, in very rich, moist garden soil. Plants can be raised from seed or started from stem cuttings—sprigs from a supermarket are easy to root. Scatter seeds or set plants against the muddy banks of a watercourse; they will grow without further attention and can be harvested as desired.

NEPETA

N. cataria (catnip, catmint)

Catnip is famous for the way its leaves and blossoms, when crushed or dried, delight cats of all sizes, from the wild mountain lion to the domestic tabby. This catnip ecstasy seems to affect only felines, but the lemony-mint-scented leaves have long been used by humans for brewing tea. The hardy perennial grows 2 to 3 feet tall and has 2- to 3-inch-long heart-shaped gray-green leaves, with downy gray undersides. They are arranged in pairs on thick, strong stems that are capped from mid- to late summer with flower spikes densely covered with small pale-pink or white blossoms. The flower spikes attract bees; in winter, goldfinches are drawn to the dry seed heads.

HOW TO GROW. Catnip grows in Zones 3–8 in any soil but prefers a moist, rich location. It thrives in partial shade, tolerates sun and can be grown from seed planted in fall or spring, although fall sowing germinates best. Sow the seeds where the plants are to grow, and when seedlings are 2 to 3 inches tall, thin them to stand 12 to 18 inches apart. Plants can also be started from root divisions in the spring. Except for weeding, catnip requires little care.

If you pinch back the plant when the first flower buds form, it will become bushy enough to produce as many as three successive harvests of leaves. To harvest, cut off the top leaves and flowers and dry them for two or three days in a shady place; then strip the leaves and flowers from the stems and store in an airtight container. Catnip seeds remain viable for four or five years.

WATERCRESS
Nasturtium officinale

CATNIP
Nepeta cataria

For climate zones and frost dates, see maps, pages 150–151.

Catnip grown indoors as a house plant needs moist but not soggy soil and at least five hours of direct sunlight a day. It does best in temperatures of 55° to 60°. Start indoor plants from seed, using a 4-inch pot filled with a commercial potting mixture supplemented with lime. Prune to preserve a bushy shape; catnip grown indoors tends to become straggly.

NIGELLA
N. sativa (fennel flower, love-in-a-mist, black cumin)

Fennel flower is a dainty annual grown as much for its beauty as for the usefulness of its seed for flavoring. It is an erect plant 12 to 15 inches high with finely cut foliage that resembles the foliage of true fennel, a different plant. In midsummer each stem is capped with a blue or white flower 1 inch across. The bulging green seed pods, which ripen in late summer, contain triangular black seeds, peppery and nutmeg-scented, that are sprinkled on breads and cakes and used as an ingredient in curries.

HOW TO GROW. Fennel flower can be grown in Zones 3–10. It needs full sun and grows well in almost any well-drained, moderately rich soil. In the fall or early spring, sow seeds outdoors where the plants are to remain; fennel flower is not easy to transplant. When plants are 2 inches tall, thin them to stand 8 to 12 inches apart. Fennel flower seeds are ready to harvest approximately four months after planting and remain viable for three years. To harvest the seeds, cut off the pods when they turn brown. Dry them in a shady, well-ventilated place. Rub the pods between your palms to free the seeds. Let the seeds dry, then store them in an airtight container. Each plant produces only a few seeds.

O

OCIMUM
O. basilicum (sweet basil); *O. basilicum* 'Dark Opal' (purple basil)

Sweet basil, a native of tropical Pacific islands, is a bushy annual, 15 to 24 inches high, whose aromatic leaves exude a pleasant fragrance even when lightly brushed. A favorite flavoring for tomatoes, sweet basil is used in quantity for a green sauce—called *pesto* in Italy and *pistou* in France—that is added to soups, vegetables, fish and pasta in Mediterranean cookery. An ornamental variety called Dark Opal is cultivated mainly for its colorful foliage, although it too is used in cooking.

The silky leaves of both sweet basil and purple basil grow 1 to 2 inches long. From midsummer on, whorls of ⅛- to ¼-inch white blossoms form on spikes at the ends of the stems of sweet basil; the flowers of purple basil are lavender. The leaves of both kinds can be harvested continuously throughout the growing season.

HOW TO GROW. Both sweet and purple basil are easily grown, warm-climate plants, sensitive to frost, that require full sun and a well-drained soil with a pH of 5.5 to 6.5, supplemented with manure or compost.

Sow the seeds outdoors when the danger of frost is past, covering them with ¼ inch of soil. When the seedlings are 2 to 3 inches tall, thin or transplant them to stand 12 inches apart. If large plants are sought early in the season, start the seeds indoors about two months before the last frost, transplanting seedlings to individual pots when they are about 1 inch tall. Basil transplants readily and grows rapidly if temperatures are 70° or above. Transfer seedlings to the garden when all danger of frost is past. Pinch off the tops when the plants are 5 to 6 inches high to encourage bushy growth. Harvest fresh leaves at any time, cutting plants to within 6 inches of the ground if desired. If such severe pruning is

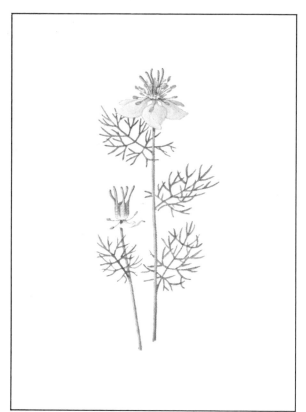

FENNEL FLOWER
Nigella sativa

SWEET BASIL
Ocimum basilicum

done to obtain a large harvest, feed the plants with 5-10-5 fertilizer applied at the rate of 3 ounces per 10 feet of row; this will help ensure several crops of leaves.

To harvest basil for drying, cut the stem just before the flowers open, strip the leaves from the stem and dry them on trays in a dark, airy place. When the leaves are dry, store them in an airtight container. Basil leaves can also be quick-frozen, or they can be immersed in olive oil, Italian style. Oil-kept leaves may blacken, but they will keep their flavor for many months.

Basil can also be grown indoors as a pot plant; purple basil is particularly suitable to this purpose, being both decorative and useful. Both types need at least five hours of direct sunlight daily or 12 hours of artificial light, and require a barely moist soil. Garden seedlings no more than 6 inches tall can be put into 6-inch pots filled with potting soil and moved indoors to a sunny window sill. Basil can also be started from seeds indoors in pots at any time of year. Feed indoor plants about once a month with an all-purpose liquid fertilizer, used at half strength.

OLIVE, SWEET See *Osmanthus*
ONION, TOP and EGYPTIAN See *Allium*
ORACH See *Atriplex*
ORANGE, CALAMONDIN See *Citrus*
OREGANO See *Origanum*

ORIGANUM

O. dictamnus, also called *Amaracus dictamnus* (dittany of Crete, hop marjoram); *O. majorana* (sweet marjoram, knotted marjoram); *O. vulgare* (wild marjoram, oregano)

The oreganos have long baffled herbalists and gardeners because their seeds look alike and so do the plants in their early stages of growth. Dittany when young is identical in appearance to wild marjoram, for instance, except for the larger size of its leaves. It also smells like wild marjoram, yet it lacks that plant's pungent taste. But unlike wild marjoram, dittany is grown chiefly for decoration, although its leaves can be eaten in salads or used as a substitute for tea; it is also one of the ingredients in vermouth. In the same way, mild-flavored sweet marjoram and strong-flavored wild marjoram are often mistakenly sold for each other because the plants resemble each other so closely. Both are cooking herbs; the latter, as oregano, is the familiar flavoring of pizzas. To complicate matters further, however, the dried oregano sold commercially for cooking is usually a Mexican variety of wild marjoram that neither tastes nor smells like the true home-grown variety.

Dittany is a tender perennial, about 12 inches tall, that produces drooping heads of tiny pink flowers during the late summer. Sweet marjoram is a tender perennial, 8 to 10 inches high, that is raised as an annual except in the mild climate of Zones 9 and 10; it produces very inconspicuous pinkish-white blossoms 10 or 12 weeks after seeds are planted. Wild marjoram, a hardy perennial, grows 2 to 2½ feet tall and produces 3- to 4-inch clusters of small, purple-pink flowers in summer and fall.

HOW TO GROW. Sweet and wild marjoram can be grown outdoors in the open garden in Zones 3–10, but dittany is usually grown in pots kept outdoors in the summer and brought indoors wherever winter temperatures fall below 45°. All three kinds of oregano need full sun and do best in light, dry, well-drained, somewhat alkaline soil with a pH between 6.0 and 8.0.

Dittany can be propagated from stem cuttings taken in the spring and rooted in the moist sand. Pot rooted cuttings in any

PURPLE BASIL
Ocimum basilicum 'Dark Opal'

DITTANY OF CRETE
Origanum dictamnus

SWEET MARJORAM
Origanum majorana

For climate zones and frost dates, see maps, pages 150–151.

WILD MARJORAM
Origanum vulgare

SWEET OLIVE
Osmanthus fragrans

commercial potting soil. Give the plants direct sunlight. Dittany should be watered well, then allowed to dry between waterings. When night temperatures remain above 45° move dittany outdoors. In the fall, cut off the flowering stems and transfer plants indoors for the winter. Water only enough to prevent wilting during the winter months. Dittany can also be grown indoors all year round; for this it requires at least five hours of direct sunlight a day. Indoors, flower buds have to be pinched off to stimulate leaf growth; the plant may flower and die if this is not done.

Both sweet marjoram and wild marjoram can be raised from seeds. The seeds germinate best when they are sown indoors in flats or cold frames in early spring for transfer outdoors when temperatures remain above 45°. They can also be sown directly in the garden when temperatures remain above 45°. Cover the seeds with no more than $^1/_{16}$ inch of soil. They usually germinate in eight to 10 days. When plants are 2 to 3 inches high, thin or transplant them to stand 8 to 15 inches apart. During the early stages of development, control weeds by cultivating around the base of plants and water only if leaves begin to wilt. When the plants are 6 inches high, pinch back the tops to encourage branching and bushy growth. Sweet marjoram can also be propagated from stem cuttings and wild marjoram can be propagated by dividing roots in spring or fall. In fact, the tangled roots of wild marjoram should be divided every two or three years to renew their vigor, since older plants are less flavorful. Both marjorams also propagate by self-seeding.

Leaves and stem tips of sweet and wild marjoram can be cut for use as soon as the plants are 4 to 5 inches high, but their flavor is best after the flower buds form, just before flowering. To harvest, cut the stem tops down to the first two sets of leaves. New stems and shoots will grow, producing second and sometimes third crops. Dry the leaves in a warm, dry, shaded place, and store them in an airtight container. Drying improves the flavor of both sweet and wild marjoram.

Sweet and wild marjorams can be grown in pots indoors. Start from either seeds or plants, and treat exactly like dittany. Pinch back stem ends to encourage bushy growth, and feed plants a standard liquid fertilizer at half strength at monthly intervals.

ORRIS See *Iris*

OSMANTHUS
O. fragrans (sweet olive)

Sweet olive is an evergreen shrub with flowers that give off a strong, pleasant, orange-like aroma. It is a native of Asia, where it grows to a height of 30 feet, but in the United States it seldom reaches a height of more than 10 feet. Its ¼-inch flowers, so tiny they are hard to see, bloom profusely in late winter and spring, and may appear intermittently at other seasons. The 2½- to 4-inch-long leaves are dark green and leathery, with smooth or finely serrated edges.

HOW TO GROW. Sweet olive grows outdoors only in Zones 9 and 10; it does best where it is shaded from the midday sun and protected from wind. It will grow in almost any well-drained soil, kept barely moist, that contains about one-third organic material such as peat moss or leaf mold. Sweet olive is generally propagated from cuttings taken in late summer. It is often grown in pots for indoor use, where its fragrance will perfume a whole room. It grows slowly indoors; even old plants rarely exceed a height of 2 or 3 feet. Do not allow the soil to dry out; it should be kept slightly moist. Feed indoor plants monthly with a house-plant fertilizer diluted to half strength, and give them bright reflected or indirect light.

OSWEGO TEA See *Monarda*

P

PAIGLE See *Primula*
PANSY, WILD See *Viola*
PARSLEY, BEAKED or FRENCH See *Anthriscus*
PARSLEY, FRENCH CURLY See *Petroselinum*
PARSLEY, ITALIAN PLAIN-LEAVED See *Petroselinum*
PASQUE FLOWER See *Anemone*

PELARGONIUM

P. 'Clorinda' (Clorinda geranium); *P. crispum* (lemon-scented geranium); *P. graveolens* (rose-scented geranium); *P. tomentosum* (peppermint-scented geranium)

Geraniums, technically pelargoniums, include many scented species and varieties whose leaves are used as herbs for flavoring beverages, preserves, desserts and other foods and, especially in combination, as ingredients for fragrant potpourri. The scents are carried by the geranium leaves, which release aromatic oils when touched—or in some cases in strong, hot sun. Like other geraniums, the ones with scented leaves are tender, shrubby plants, mostly native to southern Africa but now grown throughout the world. They bloom in spring but their flowers are generally unspectacular.

Lemon-scented geraniums are slender plants 2 to 3 feet tall that look like miniature evergreen trees. Their stiff, rough, three-lobed leaves are tiny—no larger than 1 inch across—and have curly serrated edges; they grow on 1- to 2-inch stems. Lavender flowers up to 2 inches across appear at the top of the plant, usually in clusters of two and three on 1- to 2-inch stems.

Rose-scented geraniums have hairy, upright stalks that may reach a height of 4 feet. They are topped by umbrella-like clusters of five to 10 tiny flowers of deep rose or lavender. The heart-shaped, deeply indented gray-green leaves become as much as 4 inches wide and are borne on stems up to 3 inches long.

Clorinda geranium is one of the showiest of the scented geraniums, with large clusters of rose-pink flowers streaked with orange-red. It is a sturdy trailing plant; its three-lobed, rough-textured, dusty-green leaves smell like eucalyptus.

The peppermint-scented geranium is also a trailing plant, but its velvety heart-shaped leaves, often 4 inches wide, are emerald green and appear on thick, soft, hairy stems up to 6 inches long. The few tiny flowers are white, with a red spot in the center of each; they bloom in clusters on stems that also grow as long as 6 inches.

HOW TO GROW. Although the peppermint geranium tolerates light shade, all scented geraniums do best in full sun, in well-drained soil that is slightly on the dry side. They can be grown outdoors in Zones 9 and 10, but must be potted and brought indoors in the winter in Zones 3–8. While scented geraniums can be raised from seed, the resulting plants may not bear the scent of the parent. To be sure of scented leaves, buy true-to-name varieties from geranium specialists. Although all geraniums can be propagated from root cuttings, the universal propagation method is by stem cuttings, taken at any time; they root well in barely damp, coarse sand.

Grown indoors as house plants, scented geraniums need at least four hours of direct sunlight a day, or 14 to 18 hours of artificial light. When repotting becomes necessary, use a commercial potting soil. Let the soil get barely dry before watering. If it is allowed to get very dry, the lower leaves will turn yellow and fall off. Feed with any house-plant fertilizer, used at half strength, every two weeks during the flowering season and monthly the rest of the year.

CLORINDA GERANIUM
Pelargonium 'Clorinda'

LEMON-SCENTED GERANIUM
Pelargonium crispum

For climate zones and frost dates, see maps, pages 150–151.

ROSE-SCENTED GERANIUM
Pelargonium graveolens

PEPPERMINT-SCENTED GERANIUM
Pelargonium tomentosum

PENNYROYAL See *Mentha*
PEPPER CRESS See *Lepidium*
PEPPERMINT See *Mentha*
PEPPERMINT-SCENTED GERANIUM See *Pelargonium*

PERILLA

P. frutescens crispa (purple perilla, summer coleus, beefsteak plant)

Purple perilla is grown in United States herb gardens for its ornamental foliage that gives off a spicy cinnamon-like fragrance when rubbed or bruised. In Japan the leaves, seeds and flower spikes are a basic culinary herb, *shisho*. The dark leaves with their deeply fringed edges resemble those of red coleus, hence the common name summer coleus, but in fact the two plants are unrelated. Perilla is an erect annual, 2 to 4 feet or more tall, with branching, burgundy-colored stems. The large leaves, 3 to 6 inches long, are covered on top with whitish hairs and underneath with purple ones. In late summer, the plant produces short flower spikes bearing inconspicuous pinkish-green blossoms. Most gardeners pinch out the flower spikes as they develop to encourage more of the colorful foliage on bushy plants.

HOW TO GROW. The tough, pest-free purple perilla grows in Zones 3–10. It will grow in any soil in full sun or partial shade. To achieve the earliest outdoor-grown seedlings, sow the seeds in late fall. Otherwise sow them in early spring; in either case they will not germinate until the arrival of warm weather. You can also sow seeds indoors eight to 10 weeks before outdoor night temperatures remain above 55°, then transplant them to the garden. Thin or transplant seedlings to stand 9 to 12 inches apart. When plants are 6 inches tall, pinch off the tips to stimulate branching, and repeat pinching at each 6-inch increment of growth. Perilla will die with the first frost, but if some of the flower spikes are permitted to mature, the plant will seed itself and new plants will appear the following spring.

PETROSELINUM

P. crispum (parsley, French curly parsley); *P. filicinum,* also called *P. neopolitanum* (Italian plain-leaved parsley)

Curly parsley and Italian parsley are hardy biennials but they are usually cultivated as annuals for their tender, peppery first-year leaves, much prized in cooking. Curly parsley, which has crisp, tightly curled foliage, is often used raw as a garnish. But many cooks contend that flat-leaved Italian parsley has a stronger flavor and is superior for cooking as a vegetable. The curly variety grows 10 to 12 inches tall and the Italian about 18 inches in the first year. In the second year, 2-foot-tall flower stalks appear, and their blossoms ripen into brown seeds that will remain viable for a period of two or three years.

HOW TO GROW. Parsley grows in Zones 3–10. It thrives in full sun but will tolerate very light shade and needs rich, well-drained soil with a pH of 5.0 to 7.0, supplemented with manure or compost. In most areas, sow seeds outdoors in the very early spring or in the late fall just before the soil freezes. Plant seeds ¼ inch deep. (In northern zones, seeds can be started indoors in late winter.) Parsley seeds are extremely slow to germinate, requiring four to six weeks. To speed germination in the spring, soak seeds in lukewarm water for 24 hours before planting. In areas where summer temperatures exceed 90° for prolonged periods, sow seeds in the fall. While the seeds are germinating, the bed should be watered as necessary to keep it from becoming dry. Thin seedlings to stand 3 inches apart when they are 2 to 3 inches high. Allow plants to spread until they touch, then pull and use every other plant. Continue harvesting alternate plants until they stand a foot apart. When plants reach a height of 4 inches, feed them with a 5-10-5 commercial fertilizer at the rate of 3 ounces for every 10 feet of row. Repeat this feeding a month later.

Parsley leaves can be harvested as soon as the plant is 6 inches tall. A mature plant of either variety produces about 1 cup of leaves every three weeks during the harvesting season. Leaves can be refrigerated for use fresh, or they can be frozen or even dried. To dry the leaves, spread them out on a screen in a shady and well-ventilated place. Finally, store them in an airtight container.

Both varieties of parsley can be grown indoors as pot plants; they need at least five hours of direct sunlight a day or 12 hours of artificial light, and they do best in day temperatures below 70°. Indoors, parsley can be grown in any standard potting soil. To grow parsley from seed indoors, sprinkle a half-dozen seeds in the top of a 4- to 6-inch pot filled with potting mix and moisten by setting the pot in lukewarm water. Place the pot in bright indirect light until seeds germinate. Once seedlings appear, transfer to full sun or strong light and keep the soil moist but not soggy. Do not thin plants; grown close together the six plants per pot provide a steady supply of parsley for cutting. Outdoor garden plants can be potted in late summer and brought indoors to grow on a cool, sunny window sill, where they will produce fresh leaves for harvesting all winter.

PEUCEDANUM GRAVEOLENS See *Anethum*
PHEW PLANT See *Valeriana*

PIMPINELLA

P. anisum (anise, aniseed)

Sweet-tasting, sweet-smelling anise has been grown for centuries for its licorice-flavored and licorice-scented seeds, which have been used in cakes and confections, in toiletries and medicines, and in liqueurs and cordials. The 18- to 24-inch-tall annual has two extremely different kinds of foliage: the basal leaves, about ¾ inch long, are bright green and pear-shaped with deeply notched edges; the leaves along the flower stalks are feathery and finely cut, and are sometimes used as a garnish. In midsummer, lacy white blossoms form airy umbrella-shaped clusters about 2 inches wide that ripen into small ridged seeds about ⅛ inch long.

HOW TO GROW. Anise can be grown in Zones 3–10, but it is difficult to grow in northern climates because it is slow to germinate, requiring about four months to develop, and because its delicate roots do not take kindly to transplanting. However, seeds planted indoors in peat pots eight to 10 weeks before the last frost is due can be moved to the garden without shock when the weather becomes mild. Anise needs full sun and a moderately rich garden soil with pH of 5.5 to 6.5. Seeds germinate best in a combination of cool soil and warm sun; sow them in the spring when all danger of frost is past, covering them with ¼ to ½ inch of soil. If a few fast-growing radish seeds are planted with the slower-growing anise seeds they will help to mark the place in the garden. When seedlings are 2 inches tall, thin them to stand 8 inches apart. Keep them well watered, and mound dirt around the base of the young plants to support their slender stems. If flowers and seeds weigh down the stems at a later period of growth, support them with stakes.

To harvest anise seeds, cut the plants when the stems are yellow and the seeds are gray-green. Wash the seed heads in warm water, drain on a towel and spread flat to dry in a warm, dark, well-ventilated place (seeds intended for future

PURPLE PERILLA
Perilla frutescens crispa

LEFT: ITALIAN PARSLEY   RIGHT: PARSLEY
Petroselinum felicinum   *P. crispum*

For climate zones and frost dates, see maps, pages 150–151.

133

ANISE
Pimpinella anisum

COWSLIP
Primula veris

planting need not be washed). When completely dry, rub the seed heads between the palms to remove seeds from stems; store the seeds in an airtight container.

PINEAPPLE SAGE See *Salvia*
POT MARIGOLD See *Calendula*

PRIMULA
P. veris, also called *P. officinalis* (cowslip, paigle)

A wild primrose, cowslip is a hardy perennial, growing 4 to 8 inches tall. Long oval crinkled leaves rise directly from the root, first appearing as a tight coil, then unfurling to form a rosette. The pale yellow, fragrant flowers are ⅜ to ½ inch wide. In earlier times, when the wild plant was more abundant, the blossoms were gathered to make cowslip wine.

HOW TO GROW. Cowslip can be grown in Zones 5–8 and thrives in partial shade with a rich, porous, moist, acid soil (pH 5.0 to 6.0), supplemented with compost or leaf mold. Choose a damp, shady spot where the plants will not be exposed to the midday sun. Cowslip can be started from seeds sown in a cold frame in late fall or early spring; these will blossom when they are about one year old. To ensure bloom the first year, buy nursery plants in the spring. Set the young plants 6 to 12 inches apart, being careful to cover the entire root structure and the base of the stem. Cowslip thrives on frequent watering and the soil should not be allowed to dry completely. If the summer is hot, keep the plants cool with a mulch of pine needles; in winter, protect them with a mulch of pine needles or salt hay. Cowslip can be increased by dividing the plant clumps in the spring immediately after they have flowered; this procedure also prevents overcrowding.

PUDDING GRASS See *Mentha*
PULSATILLA See *Anemone*
PURPLE BASIL See *Ocimum*

R
RADICULA See *Nasturtium*
ROMAN CHAMOMILE See *Anthemis*
RORIPA See *Nasturtium*

ROSA
R. damascena (damask rose, rose of Castile); *R. gallica* (French rose, rose of Provins)

The damask rose and French rose are hardy shrubs from whose petals and fruit, called rose hips, oils have been extracted since ancient times for use in medicines, perfumes and cooking. Both of these old roses are ancestors of many modern hybrids. *Rosa gallica* is a bush rose originally found in the Balkans and still grown there commercially for the volatile oil, attar of roses, distilled from its petals. During the Middle Ages, a rose-growing industry flourished in the small French town of Provins, inspiring *Rosa gallica*'s most frequently used common names.

The damask rose usually grows 4 to 5 feet tall and (although it is technically a bush rose) resembles a climbing rose in character. Its branches are covered with large, hooked thorns and the gray-green compound leaves are composed of five to seven toothed leaflets about 1 to 2½ inches long. Lush semidouble flowers in pink, red or white bloom in early summer. The Rose des Quatre Saisons, *R. damascena semperflorens,* also blossoms again in the fall. The popular variation *R. damascena trigintipetala,* known as the Kazanlik rose, has 30-petaled, semidouble red blossoms. Although the damask rose is only slightly fragrant when fresh, its perfume increases when its petals are dried for use in potpourri.

The French rose grows 2 to 4 feet high and has stiff stems covered with bristles but essentially thornless. Its compound leaves are composed of three to five oval-shaped leaflets with sharply toothed edges; each leaflet is deeply veined on top and has prickly hairs on the underside along the midrib. In late spring the French rose produces very fragrant flowers 1½ to 3 inches wide, whose pink to crimson petals open from a disklike center filled with conspicuous yellow stamens.

HOW TO GROW. The damask and French roses grow well in Zones 4–10 and prefer full sun and good, well-drained garden soil supplemented with compost or manure. They can be planted in the fall or spring. Choose a separate bed for them, away from the entangling roots of other shrubs and trees, and space the bushes 3 to 4 feet apart. Dig a hole 24 inches deep and wide, discarding all but the topsoil. Mix well-rotted manure, compost and topsoil and make a cone-shaped mound in the bottom of the hole. Place the rose bush on this hill, spreading the roots out as much as possible (cut off any damaged roots). Fill the space around the roots with soil halfway up; water. Continue to fill the hole, firming down the soil. After the roots of spring-planted bushes are covered, mound 6 to 8 inches of soil around the base of the shrub, removing it in about two weeks when new growth begins.

After fall planting in areas where winter temperatures go below 10°, cover the newly set plants with a protective mulch of salt hay or compost. When the ground thaws the following spring, remove this winter protection. After the bushes are established, feed them twice a year, in early spring and again in early summer, using ½ cup of 5-10-5 fertilizer scratched into the soil in a 2-foot circle around each plant. To conserve moisture, prevent weed growth, and keep the roots cool, cover the soil with a mulch of straw, leaves or grass clippings. Prune bushes every spring; first remove all the dead wood and injured branches, then trim the remaining branches. Severe pruning, however, will limit the number of flowers because the shrubs will expend their energies growing new branches. Additional bushes can be propagated from suckers taken during the spring or from stem cuttings in early summer.

To harvest rose petals, collect them when the flowers are at their height; or gather fallen petals from the gound. Spread them flat on a frame covered with porous cloth or screening, and dry them in a well-ventilated, shaded place, turning them every day. If the petals are not dry in three or four days, they can be dehydrated further in a barely warm oven—under 120°. To harvest rose hips, cut them after they have turned red in the fall.

ROSE-SCENTED GERANIUM See *Pelargonium*

ROSMARINUS
R. officinalis (rosemary)

Rosemary, the herb of remembrance, is a tender, shrubby evergreen cultivated for its richly aromatic leaves, which are used fresh or dried in cooking. A native of the Mediterranean where it grows wild on rocky hillsides, its fragrance is so intense that during the harvest season when the wind is right, it can be smelled 20 miles at sea. Rosemary usually grows 2 to 3 feet high but in Zones 9 and 10 it can become 5 to 6 feet tall. Its spiky evergreen leaves are ¾ to 2 inches long and have shiny tops with downy undersides. During the winter and early spring and infrequently at other seasons, the woody stems bear blossoms ½ inch in diameter, which are attractive to bees.

DAMASK ROSE
Rosa damascena

FRENCH ROSE
Rosa gallica

For climate zones and frost dates, see maps, pages 150–151.

ROSEMARY
Rosmarinus officinalis

FRENCH SORREL
Rumex scutatus

HOW TO GROW. Rosemary is hardy only in Zones 8–10 where it is often grown as a ground cover. Elsewhere it is grown in pots that can be taken indoors over the winter. It grows best in full sun but will tolerate partial shade, and it thrives in a well-drained soil with a pH of 6.0 to 7.5; wet soils inhibit its growth. Although rosemary can be grown from seed, germination is extremely slow and it takes as long as three years to produce a sizable plant. Consequently most gardeners buy their first plant, then start new plants from stem cuttings. For cuttings, clip a sprig of firm new growth 4 to 5 inches long from the top of the plant, strip the bottom 1½ inches of leaves, and stick the sprig in wet sand until it has rooted; roots usually form in six weeks or less. Rosemary can also be propagated by pinning down the lower rambling branches against the soil until roots form, making new plants.

When planting rosemary in the garden, space it 2 to 3 feet apart to encourage bushy growth. When planting it in a pot, choose a pot the size of the roots; rosemary does best when its roots are somewhat crowded. Use a commercial potting soil supplemented with 1 tablespoon of lime to 4 cups of soil.

Indoor-grown rosemary needs at least four hours of direct sunlight a day, or 12 hours of strong artificial light. Its soil must never be allowed to dry out completely, but it should be allowed to become moderately dry between deep waterings. Indoors, the plant grows slowly and seldom reaches a height of more than 2 feet.

Rosemary leaves can be cut for use fresh at any time. When harvested for drying, their flavor is best just before the plant blooms. Spread the cut stems on a screen and dry them in a dark, well-ventilated place; then store leaves and stems in an airtight container.

ROUND-LEAVED MINT See *Mentha*
RUE See *Ruta*

RUMEX
R. scutatus (French sorrel)

French sorrel is a hardy perennial cultivated for its light green spear-shaped leaves that have a mildly sour, lemony taste. Picked when young and tender, they add zest to salads and cooked dishes: sorrel sauce is a classic accompaniment for fish. Excessive sorrel, however, acts as a diuretic. The plant grows 18 to 24 inches high and the leaves form dense clusters of foliage. Panicles of yellow-green flowers bloom in the spring followed by reddish seeds that are great favorites of finches. Like wild dock, a close relative, French sorrel has roots that grow deep into the soil and are difficult to eradicate once established.

HOW TO GROW. French sorrel grows in Zones 3–10. It does best in sun but will tolerate partial shade; it will grow in any rich, moist soil. Sow seeds outdoors in spring, covering them with ¼ inch of soil. When the seedlings are 1 to 2 inches tall, thin or transplant them to stand 6 to 8 inches apart. Pinch off flower heads as soon as they form to encourage leaf growth and to prevent seed formation. If you do allow the plants to go to seed, be ready to pull unwanted seedlings; sorrel will quickly seed itself, sometimes producing new plants in the same year the seeds fall; it spreads rapidly and is difficult to control. In hot weather sorrel leaves may turn bitter; a mulch around the bases of the plants will help to prevent this by conserving moisture. But if bitterness should develop, the mild flavor of the leaves will return when the weather becomes cooler.

French sorrel grows well indoors provided it has at least five hours of strong direct sunlight a day and plenty of water. It should be grown in deep containers, to accommodate its long roots. Use a commercial potting soil and feed the plants with liquid fertilizer, used at half strength, every two weeks. Water plants frequently enough to keep the soil from becoming completely dry. If leaves begin to curl, check them for mites, which can be treated by washing the leaves in a mild solution of soap and water. Indoor-grown sorrel reaches a height of only 8 inches.

RUTA
R. graveolens (rue, herb of grace)

Rue is a musky-smelling, semievergreen perennial cultivated for its attractive blue-green foliage and yellow blossoms, and for its seed pods, which are often dried for use in ornamental arrangements. In Greek and Roman times it was a culinary herb, but it should not be eaten and should be planted in the garden with caution, for many people have violent reactions to it, similar to those of poison ivy, and taken internally it can be poisonous. The bushy plant, 1 to 3 feet high and wide, produces 3- to 5-inch leaves segmented into oval lobes, and ¾-inch flowers consisting of four or five wide-spreading petals; these bloom in terminal clusters from midsummer to fall.

HOW TO GROW. Rue is hardy in Zones 4–10. It thrives in full sun but will tolerate partial shade and does best in well-drained, sandy, slightly alkaline soil with a pH of 7.0 to 7.5. Sow seeds outdoors in the spring or late summer, or start seeds indoors in pots in late winter for transplanting outdoors when all danger of frost is past. Thin or transplant seedlings to stand 1 to 1½ feet apart when they are 2 to 3 inches high. After flowers bloom the first time, cut off the flower heads and spread compost or manure around the bases of the plants to encourage a second flowering. Mature rue should be trimmed back to half its size every other spring to encourage full, bushy growth. The plant will seed itself; it can also be propagated, although with considerable difficulty, from stem cuttings in early summer.

RUE
Ruta graveolens

S

SAFFLOWER See *Carthamus*
SAFFRON CROCUS See *Crocus*
SAFFRON THISTLE See *Carthamus*
SAGE, GARDEN See *Salvia*
SAGE, PINEAPPLE See *Salvia*
ST. MARY'S THISTLE See *Silybum*
ST. PATRICK'S CABBAGE See *Sempervivum*
ST. PAUL'S BETONY See *Veronica*
SALAD BURNET See *Sanguisorba*

SALVIA
S. officinalis (sage, garden sage); *S. rutilans,* also called *S. elegans* (pineapple sage)

Garden sage, a shrubby perennial whose distinctive gray-green foliage has added "sage green" to the palette of colors, makes a handsome addition to the garden and a common source of flavoring for the kitchen. Its relative, pineapple sage, is purely decorative and fragrant, its leaves emitting the scent that gives the plant its name; although it has no flavor, it is sometimes used as a garnish for fruit salads.

Garden sage reaches a height of 1½ to 2½ feet, with a tendency to sprawl if not trimmed, while pineapple sage grows as tall as 3 feet. The tiny lilac-blue flowers of garden sage bloom on terminal spikes in the summer, and its wrinkled, spear-shaped leaves, 2 to 4 inches long, grow opposite each other on stiff, hairy stems. After a plant's second year these leaves can be harvested twice and sometimes three times a season, providing a cup of leaves each time. Pineap-

SAGE
Salvia officinalis

For climate zones and frost dates, see maps, pages 150–151.

PINEAPPLE SAGE
Salvia rutilans

BURNET
Sanguisorba minor

ple sage's flower spikes are bright scarlet and bloom in the fall; its leaves are light green, pointed, oval and downy.

HOW TO GROW. Garden sage is hardy in Zones 3–10; pineapple sage is more delicate, hardy only in Zones 9 and 10. Both sages thrive in any well-drained garden soil with a pH of 5.5 to 6.5. They do best in full sun, but will also grow in light shade. Sage grown from seed takes two years to reach maturity, so it is usually purchased as nursery stock or propagated from stem cuttings in early summer. If sage is to be grown from seed, sow in the early spring, covering the seeds with ¼ inch of soil. Thin seedlings or set nursery stock to stand 1½ to 2 feet apart. Each spring, cut back the previous year's growth by half, and every four or five years, as plants get woody, divide the clumps of roots in the early spring and reset them in soil enriched with compost or manure.

Garden sage leaves can be picked any time to use fresh. To store them, harvest them in late spring and again in midsummer, cutting 6- to 8-inch pieces from the tips of the stems just as the flower buds appear. Sometimes a third harvest is also possible but, to avoid leaving the plant vulnerable to cold from Zone 6 north, do not harvest sage after early fall. To dry the leaves, hang them in the shade for about a week; then store them in airtight containers.

Garden sage does not grow well indoors, but pineapple sage makes a handsome house plant. Cut it back each year after flowering so that it does not exceed 18 inches. Keep it away from freezing windows and give it direct sunlight to encourage blooming.

SAMPHIRE See *Crithmum*

SANGUISORBA
S. minor (burnet, salad burnet)

Burnet is an old-fashioned herb whose delicate cucumber-flavored leaves were once popular in cooling drinks and are still used as a garnish in salads. It is a hardy perennial growing 1 to 2 feet high, with compound leaves about ¾ inch long, which resemble the leaves of the wild rose. They spread in a rosette from the base of the plant, forming a clump 18 to 24 inches across. In early summer thimble-shaped ½-inch tufts of greenish flowers with purple-red stamens, giving an overall reddish appearance, bloom on reddish brown stems. Burnet may spread in the garden if its seeds are allowed to ripen.

HOW TO GROW. Burnet is hardy in Zones 3–10 but is grown with difficulty in southern Florida and the Gulf Coast region due to the mild, humid winters. It is almost an evergreen, its lower leaves staying green all winter. It needs full sun and grows best in well-drained soil with a pH of 6.0 to 8.0. Sow seeds in the open ground in the late fall or early spring, covering them with ½ inch of soil. Thin seedlings to stand 12 to 15 inches apart. If the soil is rich and growth is strong, it is a good idea to divide roots and replant the divisions early each spring. To maintain a constant supply of tender young leaves for eating, cut off old foliage and flower stalks to stimulate the production of new leaves. Burnet leaves can be harvested for use fresh until covered by snow.

Burnet grown indoors as a pot plant requires at least five hours of direct sunlight a day. Start with seedlings brought in from the garden, using any commercial potting soil. Trim off old leaves from time to time to keep the plant compact. Indoor-grown burnet grows more slowly and is smaller than the garden-grown plant.

SANTOLINA
S. chamaecyparissus (lavender cotton)

Lavender cotton is a tender shrubby perennial, 1 to 2 feet tall, cultivated for its decorative, pungent, silver-gray leaves whose scent is particularly noticeable when the foliage is rubbed. The leaves are often used in sachets. The fernlike foliage, 1 to 1½ inches long, branches out to create a shrubby appearance, and bushes are often wider than they are tall. They are frequently grown as a low gray hedge or as an element in formal gardens, contrasted with the green foliage of *S. virens*. If not pruned for such purpose, lavender cotton bears ¾-inch button-shaped, yellow flowers in early summer on lanky, leafless stems.

HOW TO GROW. Lavender cotton is hardy in Zones 7–10, and elsewhere is treated as an annual. It needs full sun and will grow in almost any well-drained soil. It resists salt and is an excellent seashore plant. Lavender cotton is easily propagated from stem cuttings taken in the summer, nurtured indoors over the winter and set outside the following spring. Stem cuttings are slow to reach full size, taking as long as two years to mature. Larger plants of lavender cotton can be produced by layering stems in the fall and dividing the rooted stems in the spring. Mature plants should be clipped back 50 per cent or more annually in the spring, and if the plants are being grown solely for their foliage, again in midsummer to prevent flowering. In regions where winter temperatures remain below 0° for extended periods, protect the plants with a leaf or marsh-hay mulch.

Lavender cotton grown indoors as a pot plant needs at least five hours a day of direct sunlight and good ventilation. It tolerates temperatures as low as freezing and does well in any commercial potting soil. Indoors, plants can be trained to form miniature bushes, but they require regular pruning to retain compactness; they rarely grow more than 10 to 12 inches high indoors. Allow the soil to become nearly dry between waterings, and avoid crowding next to other plants.

LAVENDER COTTON
Santolina chamaecyparissus

SATUREIA
S. hortensis (summer savory), *S. montana* (winter savory)

Summer savory and winter savory are two popular peppery-tasting seasoning herbs used to flavor meats, sauces and stuffings and to diminish the unpleasant odors of strong-smelling vegetables like turnips, Brussels sprouts and cabbage. The two savories resemble each other with their straggly, bushlike growth and weak, woody, branching stems. Both bear whorls of tiny pink, blue-lavender or white flowers from midsummer to fall, luring bees with their fragrant blossoms. The tangy flavor and scent of the savories, however, are strongest before the flowers appear.

Summer savory, an annual, is sweeter tasting and less piquant than its perennial relative, winter savory. Its narrow, lance-shaped leaves, ½ to 1½ inches long, are covered with short, downy hairs and grow sparsely in pairs along stems 12 to 18 inches high. Unless harvested, this foliage turns red deepening to purple in late summer. Summer savory is commonly picked in the summer before its flowers open; a single mature plant will yield about ¼ cup of leaves the first cutting and much less the second harvest.

Winter savory, a perennial, is a slightly smaller and wider plant than summer savory. It reaches a height of 6 to 12 inches and sprawls to an equal width. Its narrow, pointed leaves, only ¹/₁₆ inch wide, are smooth and shiny, and its flowers tend to be deeper hued than those of summer savory. The leaves, which remain green throughout the winter in mild climates, can be harvested several times and a mature plant produces ¼ cup of leaves.

HOW TO GROW. Summer and winter savory both like full sun and ordinary, not particularly fertile, well-drained soil.

SUMMER SAVORY
Satureia hortensis

For climate zones and frost dates, see maps, pages 150–151.

WINTER SAVORY
Satureia montana

HOUSELEEK
Sempervivum tectorum

Start summer savory from seeds sown about ¼ inch deep in the early spring, and for a constant supply of fresh herb, make successive plantings at three- to four-week intervals. Germination takes about 14 to 21 days. Thin seedlings to stand 4 to 6 inches apart; close spacing helps to keep the top-heavy plants from falling over. Later, when the plants are taller, mound soil around their bases to keep them upright. Fresh leaves can be cut for use at any time.

Winter savory is hardy in Zones 5–10. Its seeds are slow to germinate, so the plants are commonly started from root divisions or stem cuttings made in the spring or by layering. Set plants in the ground in early spring, spacing them 12 inches apart. When they are 6 inches tall, pinch back tops to encourage bushy growth. Remove dead wood whenever it appears, and in the fall in Zones 5 and 6 clip back the plants to 3 to 6 inches above the ground; cover each plant with a mulch of salt hay after the ground freezes. Winter savory plants need to be divided and replanted every two or three years to achieve satisfactory growth.

Both summer and winter savory should be harvested for drying before the flowers bloom. Cut summer savory down to the ground or pull it up by the roots; cut only the tender tip growth of winter savory. Hang both types upside down in bunches to dry in a brown paper bag, or lay them flat on a screen in a dark, well-ventilated room. When the leaves are thoroughly dry, rub the bag so the leaves fall to the bottom; or rub the leafstalks between the hands. Store them in an airtight container.

Both summer and winter savory can be grown indoors in pots or window boxes provided they get at least five hours of direct sunlight a day. Start with young plants or bring mature plants in from the garden in late summer. Use a standard commercial potting soil. At the time of potting, cut back winter savory to half its size, and allow it to recover outdoors for two or three weeks. Allow the soil around both savories to become moderately dry between waterings, and feed them an all-purpose fertilizer, used half strength, at three- or four-week intervals. Leaves may be cut as needed but winter savory should be trimmed sparingly in the winter because its rate of recovery after pruning is slower then.

SAVORY, SUMMER See *Satureia*
SAVORY, WINTER See *Satureia*
SEA FENNEL See *Crithmum*
SEA PURSLANE See *Atriplex*

SEMPERVIVUM

S. tectorum (houseleek, hen-and-chickens, St. Patrick's cabbage)

The houseleek is a succulent perennial formerly grown as a home remedy for warts and planted on rooftops in the belief that it prevented lightning and thunder. The fleshy wedge-shaped leaves edged with bristly white hairs form small cabbage-like rosettes 2 to 4 inches across. Each mature rosette is surrounded by smaller ones that arise as offshoots, hence the common name, hen-and-chickens. These moisture-storing leaves enable the plants to survive during the driest weather. In midsummer, a flower spike rises from the center of each mature rosette, reaching a height of about 9 inches. As the pinkish-red blooms fade, the main rosette dies, but new rosettes continue to grow to keep a colony of plants thriving for many years.

HOW TO GROW. Houseleek grows in Zones 3–10 except on the humid Gulf Coast. It needs well-drained soil. It is usually planted in rock gardens or along borders. You can plant offsets at any time, spacing them 6 to 9 inches apart; plants spread quickly through new offsets to fill open spaces. Fertilizer is rarely needed and may even cause abnormal growth.

Houseleek can be grown indoors like cactus in a sunny window. Plant it in a commercial potting soil formulated for cactus or mix equal parts potting soil and coarse sand. Keep the soil barely moist during the active growing season, and allow it to become nearly dry during the winter rest period.

SENNA, WILD See *Cassia*

SESAMUM
S. indicum, also called *S. orientale* (sesame, benne)

Sesame is a tropical annual cultivated in Asia and Africa for its oil and for its oily, nut-flavored seeds, which are used whole, in cakes and cookies, or ground, as an ingredient in Middle Eastern cooking. Sesame reaches a height of 1 or 2 feet, and its leaves are 3 to 5 inches long. Throughout the summer it produces 1-inch-long trumpet-shaped white flowers with pink, yellow or pale violet markings. The seed pods form inside the faded flowers and when fully ripened suddenly burst open, scattering the seeds. (The magic password "open sesame," used by Ali Baba in the *Arabian Nights* tale, probably originated from this trait.) A single plant yields 1 tablespoon of sesame seeds and can only be harvested once.

HOW TO GROW. A native and staple of India and Africa, sesame needs approximately 120 days of hot weather for the seeds to mature, so the plant is usually grown only in Zones 7–10. Sesame needs full sun, but will grow in almost any well-drained soil. Sow seeds ¼ inch deep in late spring when night temperatures remain above 60°, or sow indoors in pots or flats six to eight weeks before this date, for transfer to the open garden. Thin seedlings or transplant pot-grown plants to stand 6 to 8 inches apart. To harvest, cut the stems off at the ground before the oldest pods begin to open and drop them in a paper bag until the seed pods dry and release their seeds. Store the seeds in an airtight container.

SHALLOT See *Allium*
SHOO-FLY See *Baptisia*

SILYBUM
S. marianum (St. Mary's thistle, holy or milk thistle)

St. Mary's thistle, a biennial once valued as an herb and a vegetable, has maintained a place in the garden as an exotic foliage plant. Its large, deeply cut, spine-edged shiny green leaves, 12 to 15 inches long, are crisscrossed on the surface with a tracery of thick white veins. In midsummer of the second year, if the flower stems are not cut back, the plant produces thistle-like blossoms, 1 to 2 inches across, on stalks 2 to 4 feet high. Like other biennials, St. Mary's thistle dies after flowering, but it seeds itself and new plants appear the following spring.

HOW TO GROW. St. Mary's thistle is hardy in Zones 8–10, thriving in full sun and ordinary garden soil. Sow seeds in early spring where the plants are to remain, and thin seedlings to stand about 2 feet apart. If the flowering stem is removed before the blossom opens, St. Mary's thistle can sometimes be forced to grow as a foliage plant beyond its normal two-year life cycle.

SINAPIS See *Brassica*
SISYMBRIUM See *Nasturtium*

SIUM
S. sisarum (skirret)

Skirret is a perennial with a multiple root that tastes

SESAME
Sesamum indicum

ST. MARY'S THISTLE
Silybum marianum

SKIRRET
Sium sisarum

WOOD BETONY
Stachys officinalis

something like parsnip and is sometimes grown as a vegetable. It reaches a height of 2 to 4 feet and has sharply toothed compound leaves having three to seven leaflets, ½ to 1 inch long. In early summer it bears umbrella-shaped heads of tiny white flowers about 1 inch across. The long tapering roots grow in clusters like dahlias but are joined at the top. One plant produces many roots.

HOW TO GROW. Skirret is hardy in Zones 4–6 and does best in a rich, well-drained garden soil with a pH of 6.0 to 8.0. Although it can be started from seeds sown ½ inch deep in the spring or fall, the easiest way to grow skirret is from root divisions, planted in the early spring and spaced 8 to 12 inches apart. If growing skirret for table use, cut back the flower heads before they turn to seed to encourage root growth. Since the roots will withstand freezing, they will not be harmed by remaining in the ground, like parsnips, although they can also be dug up and stored in sand.

SKIRRET See *Sium*
SON-BEFORE-THE-FATHER See *Tussilago*
SORREL, FRENCH See *Rumex*
SPANISH LAVENDER See *Lavandula*
SPEARMINT See *Mentha*
SPEEDWELL, COMMON See *Veronica*
SPINACH, FRENCH See *Atriplex*
SPIRAEA See *Filipendula*
SPOTTED DEAD-NETTLE See *Lamium*

STACHYS
S. officinalis (wood betony, bishop's wort, woundwort); *S. olympica*, also called *S. lanata* (lamb's ears, woolly betony, donkey's ears)

During the Middle Ages these two perennial herbs were grown for their large leaves that were used for bandaging wounds, hence the name woundwort. Today both are cultivated for their ornamental value—wood betony for its flowers, lamb's ears as a ground cover. Except for the fact that their flowers bloom on spikes, the two plants do not at all resemble each other.

Wood betony grows 1 to 3 feet tall and its hairy, heart-shaped leaves are 2 to 4 inches long with deeply wrinkled surfaces and coarse-toothed edges. In midsummer it produces flowering spikes densely filled with bell-shaped blossoms that are good for cutting. The triangular seeds, enclosed in brown pods that drop to the ground, seed themselves in the fall. The entire plant is strongly aromatic.

Lamb's ears, a smaller plant 1 to 1½ feet tall, is named for its soft, downy foliage that strongly resembles the silky texture of young animal ears. The texture of these large, elongated, gray-green leaves, 3 to 6 inches long and 1 to 1½ inches wide, comes from a covering of soft woolly hairs. The flower spikes of lamb's ears, which bloom in early summer, rise about 6 inches above the foliage on fat stems; unlike those of wood betony, they are not striking.

HOW TO GROW. Both herbs can be grown in Zones 3–10 except in southern Florida and along the Gulf Coast, where they are cultivated with difficulty because of the area's humid winters. They thrive in full sun and a well-drained garden soil. Although they may be started from seeds sown in the spring, the plants take two years to mature. Consequently they are usually grown from root divisions planted in the early spring or fall, spaced 12 to 18 inches apart. Plants spread to form a compact mass and need little care. If the flowering spikes are cut back after blossoming, new blossoms will keep reappearing up until the first frost. Divide plant clumps every two or three years to prevent overcrowding.

STAR FLOWER See *Borago*
SUCCORY See *Cichorium*
SUMMER COLEUS See *Perilla*
SUMMER SAVORY See *Satureia*
SWEET BALM See *Melissa*
SWEET BASIL See *Ocimum*
SWEET BAY See *Laurus*
SWEET FLAG See *Acorus*
SWEET MARJORAM See *Origanum*
SWEET OLIVE See *Osmanthus*
SWEET VIOLET See *Viola*
SWEET WOODRUFF See *Asperula*

SYMPHYTUM

S. officinale (comfrey, knitbone, blackwort, boneset)

Comfrey is a hardy perennial used to brew an herbal tea; the young leaves can be eaten, combining the flavors of endive and asparagus. Farmers, especially in Europe, also grow comfrey for composting, plowing it back as enrichment for the soil. It is a sturdy plant, reaching a height of 2 to 3½ feet with very large, hairy lower leaves, as much as 15 to 20 inches long; the leaves grow smaller in size higher up the flower-bearing stem. Beginning in late spring, ¾-inch-long well-shaped flowers of yellow, mauve, blue or white bloom in arched sprays on slender stems and keep blooming for most of the summer. Each flower produces four seeds which ripen in a cup-shaped fruit.

HOW TO GROW. Comfrey is hardy in Zones 3–10. It does best in full sun but tolerates partial shade; it thrives in any moist, fairly rich garden soil. It is usually grown from root divisions or from root cuttings taken in the spring or fall. Plant the root sections horizontally, 3 to 6 inches deep and 3 to 4 feet apart, away from smaller herbs. To encourage leaf growth, cut off the flower sprays when they appear. Although leaves may be harvested from the first year on, the best yields are in the third year. Cut leaves when the plants are 12 to 18 inches high, just before they bloom. Cut no lower than 2 inches from the ground, so as not to injure the root crown of the plant. Fresh leaves are most desirable, but leaves may be dried for later use; dry them for 2 or 3 days in a cool, dark place, then crush them between your palms and store them in an airtight container.

T

TANACETUM

T. vulgare, also called *Chrysanthemum vulgare* (tansy, bitter buttons, alecost)

Tansy is a hardy perennial 2 to 5 feet tall whose pungent, bitter-tasting leaves were formerly used to flavor foods, but it is dangerous if taken internally except in extremely small quantities and is considered a poisonous drug. Today it is grown in the garden for dried flower arrangements. It is a decorative plant, admired for its deeply cut fernlike leaves, 3 to 5 inches long, and for its clusters of yellow, button-shaped petalless flowers, ¼ inch wide, which bloom in mid- to late summer. The flowers are long-lasting and so are the flat-topped seed heads that follow them; they remain on the plant through the winter, and seed themselves the following spring. In the garden tansy can be aggressive, its creeping roots quickly taking over more space than was originally allotted to the plant.

HOW TO GROW. Tansy is hardy throughout the United States and is often seen along the roadside growing as a weed. It does best in full sun but will tolerate shade; although it will grow in almost any soil, it is especially luxuriant in a relatively moist, loamy soil. Sow seeds in early

LAMB'S EARS
Stachys olympica

COMFREY
Symphytum officinale

For climate zones and frost dates, see maps, pages 150–151.

TANSY
Tanacetum vulgare

DANDELION
Taraxacum officinale

GERMANDER
Teucrium chamaedrys

spring or late fall, or start plants from root divisions in the early spring, spacing plants 12 to 24 inches apart. Place tansy against a wall or fence to help protect the long stems from blowing over in wind and rain; if not grown against a fence, mature plants may need to be staked. Because tansy spreads rapidly, it should be given an isolated position or should be planted in a sunken open-ended metal barrel that will constrict the wandering roots. If the flower heads are cut off before they seed, tansy can be encouraged to produce a hedgelike growth. To dry the flowers for winter arrangements, snip off the yellow buttons just after they have opened, and hang them in loose bunches upside down in a cool, dark place with good ventilation.

TANSY See *Tanacetum*

TARAXACUM
T. officinale (dandelion)

Suggested to gardeners with misgivings, this well-known weed, so often considered a troublesome pest in the garden and lawn, is actually a valuable salad herb, rich in vitamins A, B, C and D. In France, the young, tender leaves are especially popular, and the root—like the root of its close relative chicory—is roasted as an additive for coffee.

Dandelion is a perennial 2 to 12 inches tall whose deeply serrated, dark green leaves inspired the French name "dent de lion," or lion's tooth. Its golden yellow flowers, among the first to appear in the spring, bloom on solitary, hollow stems, and quickly turn to fluffy puffballs, scattering hundreds of seeds in the wind. Seeds germinate in only three days, which explains the plant's rapid proliferation. The deep-reaching taproot is difficult to eradicate and its removal requires special tools or weed killers.

HOW TO GROW. Dandelion is hardy throughout the United States and adapts to any soil conditions including very poor ones. However, to produce the most tender leaves, plant dandelions in rich, moist soil. Although some seed catalogs do include selected, large-leaved types of dandelion, wild specimens are not difficult to find. Sow dandelion seeds in the spring or fall in an isolated part of the garden where they can be controlled, or transplant clumps to a spot where they can be kept under cultivation. Cut flower heads before they open to increase the plant's production of salad greens. The tender leaves can be cut at any time, but their flavor is best in the spring when they first appear. One plant may be harvested several times during its five-month growing season.

TARRAGON, FRENCH See *Artemisia*
TEA JASMINE See *Jasminum*
TEASEL See *Dipsacus*

TEUCRIUM
T. chamaedrys (germander, chamaedrys, wall germander)

Once highly esteemed as a treatment for gout, germander is grown today as a ground cover or border plant. It spreads rapidly from creeping roots and rises above the ground in tufts only 6 to 18 inches high. Its woody, branching upright stems bear shiny, dark green oval leaves, ½ to 1½ inches long, scalloped along the edge and covered with tiny hairs. The ¾-inch speckled flowers are tubular, with upper and lower lips. They grow in whorls consisting of about six blossoms at the point where the leaves join the stem, and bloom in late summer. Germander is often planted as a low hedge because it responds well to shearing.

HOW TO GROW. Germander is hardy in Zones 5–10. It does best in full sun but will tolerate partial shade and thrives on any well-drained, fairly rich, light-textured soil. Seeds are extremely slow to germinate, taking up to 30 days, so the easiest way to propagate germander is from stem cuttings. Plants can also be propagated from root divisions. Set rooted cuttings or root divisions in the garden in the spring, spacing them 12 inches apart along a border, or tuck individual plants into wall crevices or between paving stones. Cut back the leaf tips and woody stems every spring—this pruning will encourage new growth.

THIMBLE FLOWER See *Digitalis*
THISTLE, BLESSED See *Cnicus*
THISTLE, ST. MARY'S, HOLY or MILK See *Silybum*

THYMUS

T. citriodorus (lemon thyme); *T. serpyllum* (wild thyme, mother-of-thyme, creeping thyme); *T. vulgaris* (common thyme, garden thyme, black thyme)

An essential ingredient in the cook's most basic *bouquet garni,* thyme has been cultivated since the days of ancient Greece for its strongly aromatic, slightly pungent foliage. The low, shrubby perennials in this large genus of more than 100 species vary from 1 to 12 inches in height and can be differentiated by the size and intensity of their scented leaves and the upright or reclining position of their stems. All thymes have thin, woody, twiglike stems with small, shiny oval-shaped leaves approximately ¼ to ½ inch long. In the early summer, pale rose to lilac-colored flowers appear at the ends of the stems or in whorls where the upper leaves join the stem. The tiny, round seeds keep their germinating power for up to three years.

Common thyme and lemon thyme are popular for cooking while wild thyme is chiefly grown as an ornamental garden herb. Common thyme, the tallest of the three, also has the strongest scent and flavor; it forms upright bushes 6 to 12 inches high. There are three principal varieties of common thyme: English or variegated-leaf thyme; German or broad-leaf thyme; and French summer or narrow-leaf thyme. Each of these varieties is distinguished, as its name indicates, by the shape of its leaves.

Lemon thyme closely resembles common thyme except for its intense lemon scent. Its leaves are slightly broader and its stems semitrailing. One variety of lemon thyme has yellowish-green leaves and grows only 6 inches high; it is used as a fragrant ground cover.

Wild thyme, often called mother-of-thyme because it is thought to be one of the original thymes, is a creeping, delicate-appearing but tough species cultivated for its aromatic carpet-like growth, which is especially suited to rock gardens and terraces; its tiny, erect flowering stems rise only 1 to 3 inches high. The numerous varieties of wild thyme differ in flower color and the size and shape of the leaves, including tiny white *T.s. albus,* the lavender-flowered *T.s. aureus,* the crimson-blossomed *T.s. coccineus* and the woolly gray-leafed *T.s. lanuginosus.*

HOW TO GROW. Except for wild thyme, which does not thrive in the humidity of the Gulf states, thymes grow throughout the United States, and do well indoors. They thrive on full sun and grow best in light, well-drained soil with a pH of 5.5 to 7.0. Plants can be grown from seeds sown ¼ inch deep outdoors in the spring or started indoors in pots or flats. But germination is slow—thyme requires about two years to reach usable size—and so this herb is commonly grown from root divisions made in the spring or stem cuttings taken any time. Wild thyme can, in addition, be propagated by layering. Space common and lemon thymes 12 inches

LEMON THYME
Thymus citriodorus

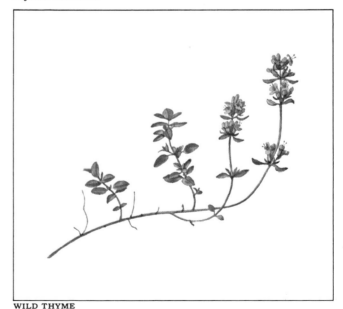

WILD THYME
Thymus serpyllum

For climate zones and frost dates, see maps, pages 150–151.

COMMON THYME
Thymus vulgaris

FENUGREEK
Trigonella foenum-graecum

apart; tuck wild thyme between rocks, bricks or flagstones, or if using it as a ground cover, space plants 10 inches apart. Scatter a tablespoon of cottonseed or bone meal around the base of each plant and scratch this supplement into the soil. Do not feed again until the following spring because fast growth makes plants susceptible to winterkill.

In early spring, trim the stems of lemon and common thyme back to half of the previous year's growth to encourage dense growth. In areas where winter temperatures remain below zero for extended periods, sprinkle a winter mulch of salt hay over the plants in the late fall after the ground freezes. Thyme becomes woody and less fragrant after several years unless young growth is encouraged by spring pruning.

Leaves can be picked in small quantities for fresh use at any time. To harvest the herb for drying, cut the stems back just before or at the time of flowering and hang upside down in bunches to dry in a dark, well-ventilated place at temperatures under 100°. Strip the leaves from the stems when dry and store in an airtight container. The flowers can also be dried for fragrant sachets and potpourris. When harvesting thyme in late summer, do not remove more than a third of the stem, so the plant will not be encouraged to make tender growth that may not survive the winter.

Lemon and common thymes grown indoors as pot plants require at least five hours of strong, direct sunlight a day. They do best in potting soils that approximate their gravelly outdoor environment and a standard commercial potting soil should be supplemented with lime chips or coarse sand. Plant several containers of different varieties for a steady supply of kitchen thyme, choosing pots according to the size of the plants. Keep the stem tips well pruned to encourage a bushy growth. Wild thyme usually does not thrive indoors. Water all plants until moist but not soggy, and allow the soil to dry between waterings.

TOP ONION See *Allium*

TRIGONELLA

T. foenum-graecum (fenugreek, bird's-foot, Greek hayseed)

One of the oldest and most widely used herbs, fenugreek is cultivated for its celery-flavored seeds, which are an ingredient in curries and chutneys, in the Middle Eastern candy halvah, and in an imitation maple syrup sold in Europe.

Fenugreek is an annual and a member of the pea family. It grows 1 to 2 feet tall and its 1- to 2-inch oval leaves are attached in groups of three to upright, hollow stems. In its early stages of growth the plant resembles sweet clover. Beginning early in the summer and continuing for several months, very fragrant off-white flowers, ½ to 1 inch long, bloom at the joining of the leaf with the stem. These are followed by pointed seed pods up to 6 inches long, which resemble string beans but grow upright; each pod contains about 16 brown seeds.

HOW TO GROW. Fenugreek adapts to any well-drained, loamy garden soil; it needs full sun. Sow seeds in the spring when danger of frost is past, covering them with ¼ inch of soil. Thin seedlings to stand 4 inches apart. Plants will bear fruit in about four months. To harvest, uproot the plants when the pods are brown and hang them upside down to dry in a warm, shady spot. Remove the dried seeds from the pods and store them in an airtight container.

TROPAEOLUM

T. majus (nasturtium, Indian cress)

Nasturtium is a decorative climbing annual cultivated for

its spicy, peppery-tasting leaves, seeds and flowers. The leaves are eaten like watercress; the flowers are used as a garnish for salads; the pickled buds and seeds are substituted for capers. The large, round, smooth-surfaced leaves, 2 to 7 inches in diameter, have long, soft stems. They curl around any object they contact, holding the plant as it grows, sometimes as high as 6 to 10 feet. Dwarf nasturtiums may grow only 12 to 15 inches tall. Spurred flowers 1 to 2½ inches wide blossom in many colors—orange, yellow, creamy white, scarlet, salmon, cerise and mahogany. They bloom continuously from early summer on, until they are cut down by frost. The flowers are followed by seeds that grow encased three to a pod.

HOW TO GROW. Nasturtium needs full sun and thrives in practically any soil. However, rich, moist soil encourages more leaf growth, a poor, well-drained one more flowers and seeds. Nasturtium seeds germinate in about a week, but they can be speeded by soaking in lukewarm water overnight before planting. Sow seeds outdoors in early spring after the danger of frost is past, covering them with ¾ to 1 inch of soil. Or start them in peat pots in a cold frame or on a window sill to be transplanted outdoors. When the seedlings are 2 to 3 inches high, thin or transplant them to stand about 6 inches apart for dwarf varieties, 12 inches apart for climbing types. Nasturtiums attract aphids; if the leaves are to be harvested for salads, avoid chemical sprays and wash the insect pests away with a garden hose. Leaves may be cut at any time after plants are established, but are most tender before the plants flower. Seeds are gathered when the seed pods are still green, and may be pickled in various ways. The simplest way is to place them in a jar and cover them with boiled cider vinegar.

Nasturtiums do well indoors provided they have at least four hours of direct sunlight a day, and temperatures that range from 40° to 45° at night to no more than 68° during the day. Plant three seeds in a 4- to 6-inch pot filled with commercial potting soil and cover them with a thin layer of soil. Keep the soil barely moist. If plants are grown for their leaves, fertilize every two weeks with a liquid fertilizer used half strength. For flowering plants, feed monthly.

TRUE LAVENDER See *Lavandula*

TUSSILAGO

T. farfara (coltsfoot, foalfoot, son-before-the-father)

Coltsfoot is a curious plant whose flowers bloom and wither long before the first leaves appear. This growth pattern leads to the strange medieval name son-before-the-father. It is a hardy perennial that grows wild throughout Europe and the Northeastern states. In early spring it produces flat, dandelion-like flowers about 1 inch across that open only on sunny days and ripen into tufted balls that disperse their seeds on the wind. The stems are thick and scaly and grow 3 to 6 inches tall; the leaves that follow the flowers have soft, downy undersides and are shaped like hoofprints.

HOW TO GROW. Coltsfoot thrives in full sun and adapts to almost any soil condition. It should be introduced in the garden with caution, for it has creeping roots, spreads rapidly and can be difficult to eradicate. Coltsfoot can be grown from seeds or root cuttings planted in the early spring or fall. When seedlings are 2 to 3 inches high, thin them to stand 6 to 8 inches apart. To get the sturdiest plants, divide the roots every three to four years and replant them in enriched soil.

U

UPLAND CRESS See *Barbarea*

NASTURTIUM
Tropaeolum majus

COLTSFOOT
Tussilago farfara

For climate zones and frost dates, see maps, pages 150–151.

VALERIAN
Valeriana officinalis

GREAT MULLEIN
Verbascum thapsus

V

VALERIANA

V. officinalis (valerian, garden heliotrope, phew plant)

Valerian, a hardy perennial, was once grown for its strong-smelling carrot-shaped root, which attracts animals, especially rats, and according to legend was the secret ingredient carried by the Pied Piper of Hamlin. From the root's smell comes one of valerian's common names, phew plant.

Valerian is often included in perennial borders. It grows 3 to 5 feet tall, producing a clump of feathery foliage 10 inches wide from which rise hollow flower stems bearing flat-topped clusters of fragrant tiny pink flowers that smell like heliotrope. The flowers, which blossom in early summer, often do not appear on seedlings until the second year of growth when the plants mature.

HOW TO GROW. Valerian is hardy in Zones 3–10 and does well in full sun or partial shade. Although it grows best in rich, moist garden soil supplemented with compost, it tolerates almost any soil. Valerian can be started from seeds sown in spring or fall. Do not cover the seeds—simply press them against damp soil. Most gardeners buy their first plants, then propagate by division of the roots. Space plants in the garden 15 to 18 inches apart. After the flowers bloom, cut off the seed heads to keep plants from seeding themselves and to encourage root growth. After three years of flowering, valerian should be dug up, divided and replanted in enriched soil.

VERBASCUM

V. thapsus (great mullein, Aaron's rod, Jacob's staff)

A majestic biennial herb, great mullein towers 3 to 6 feet tall and is valued in the garden as a stately background plant. Since ancient times, the leaves and flowers have been used for dyes, herbal teas and dressings for wounds, and the entire plant has been set afire and carried as a torch in funeral processions.

In the first year of growth, large, woolly, 6- to 18-inch-long leaves spread out in a wide rosette at ground level, forming a gray-green ground cover that lasts through the winter; the leaves are covered on both sides with long, downy hairs. In the second year, stout spires of ¾- to 1-inch-wide yellow blossoms with protruding orange stamens rise above the ground foliage from late spring into midsummer. Their rigid, erect appearance inspired the popular names Aaron's rod and Jacob's staff. Great mullein's flowers attract bees.

HOW TO GROW. Great mullein is hardy in Zones 4–10. It needs full sun and a location sheltered from strong winds; it tolerates poor soil but does best in well-drained alkaline soil; in northern areas, where the soil freezes in the winter, good drainage is essential. Seeds must be sown in the late summer or early fall where plants are to remain because the rosette clumps cannot be transplanted successfully. Thin the seedlings to stand 2 feet apart.

VERBENA, LEMON See *Lippia*

VERONICA

V. officinalis (common speedwell, St. Paul's betony)

The creeping stems and delicate pale blue blossoms of speedwell have made it a popular ground cover. This tiny perennial has prostrate hairy branches 2 to 18 inches long with oval, tooth-edged leaves ¼ to 1 inch long. Its flowering stalks, 1 to 2½ inches long, jut upward at the junction of leaf and stem in early summer.

HOW TO GROW. Speedwell grows in Zones 3–10 except in Florida and along the Gulf Coast. It does best in dry, well-drained soils and thrives in full sun, but will grow in partial shade. It grows wild over much of eastern North America. Start plants from seeds, stem cuttings or root divisions in the spring, spacing plants or thinning seedlings to stand about 1 foot apart. Nip off faded blossoms to encourage new flowers and additional growth. Divide root clumps every three or four years in the spring or fall to prevent overcrowding.

VIOLA
V. odorata (sweet violet, florist's violet); *V. tricolor* (Johnny-jump-up, heart's ease, wild pansy)

Although they belong to the same plant family, the sweet violet and Johnny-jump-up are admired for different reasons. Sweet violet is one of the most fragrant of flowers. Its scent is an ingredient of perfumes and potpourri, and the flower itself is candied for use as a confection or a cake decoration. Johnny-jump-up is cultivated for its bright tricolored flowers, which bloom profusely in spring and summer. Sweet violet is a perennial with creeping roots; it grows 6 to 8 inches high and produces heart-shaped crinkly leaves, 2½ inches across. Deep violet, pink or white flowers, ¾ inch across, bloom from mid- to late spring. Johnny-jump-up is a biennial that seeds itself each year and therefore, once planted, is a permanent element in the garden; in fact, it has great tenacity. The plant, 3 to 8 inches high, blooms from mid-spring through late summer, and apart from its colorful ¾-inch flowers is notable for its leaves; on a single stem they can be heart-shaped, notched, lance-shaped or feathery.

HOW TO GROW. Sweet violet grows in Zones 6–10; Johnny-jump-up grows in Zones 3–10. Sweet violet thrives in any moderately rich, moist, well-drained soil supplemented with compost, manure or leaf mold; it is a woodland plant and does best in partial shade. Johnny-jump-up is a meadow plant and thrives on bright sun; it grows in almost any soil and any location, from windswept dunes to rocky uplands. Although both can be started from seed sown ⅛ inch deep, neither will bloom until the second year. Set out plants in the early spring, placing Johnny-jump-ups 4 to 6 inches apart, sweet violets 10 to 12 inches apart. Keep the soil moist but not soggy until the plants are established. During the winter, protect them with a mulch of leaves or pine needles. To propagate sweet violets, divide root clumps late in the spring after flowering or remove rooted runners in early spring. Harvest sweet violets when the flowers first open and their fragrance is strongest. Dry them in a shady, well-ventilated place and store them in an airtight container.

W

WALL GERMANDER See *Teucrium*
WATERCRESS See *Nasturtium*
WILD ARTICHOKE See *Cynara*
WILD INDIGO See *Baptisia*
WILD PANSY See *Viola*
WILD SENNA See *Cassia*
WILD THYME See *Thymus*
WINTER CRESS See *Barbarea*
WINTER SAVORY See *Satureia*
WITLOOF CHICORY See *Cichorium*
WOAD See *Isatis*
WOOD or WOOLLY BETONY See *Stachys*
WOODRUFF See *Asperula*
WORMWOOD See *Artemisia*
WOUNDWORT See *Stachys*

Y

YARROW See *Achillea*
YELLOW ROCKET See *Barbarea*

COMMON SPEEDWELL
Veronica officinalis

SWEET VIOLET
Viola odorata

JOHNNY-JUMP-UP
Viola tricolor

For climate zones and frost dates, see maps, pages 150–151.

Appendix

Climate zones and frost dates

Although many herbs are simple plants that grow wild in various corners of the earth, they are often introduced into gardens where climate conditions are quite unlike those of their native habitat. The maps on these pages, used in conjunction with the information on climate given under each plant's encyclopedia entry, will help you to determine which plants grow well in your region, when to sow seeds and set out seedlings, and when to bring in the harvest—or to pot up the growing plant for winter use indoors.

The zone map gives the average minimum winter temperatures for various regions of the United States and Canada; the zone numbers are those used in the encyclopedia entries. If you live in Cincinnati, Zone 6, for example, you will find that most of the standard culinary herbs thrive in your region, but that you had best bring rosemary indoors for the winter.

The frost maps at right, which show the first and last dates when night temperatures can be expected to fall below 32°, are helpful in determining not only when it is safe to plant tender herbs outdoors, but when to start seeds indoors for such long-germinating herbs as parsley. Similarly, the date of the first frost alerts you to the need for providing protection for tender plants.

Specific frost dates vary widely within each region, of course, even within a neighborhood—so it is advisable to check with your weather bureau for more precise local figures and to keep a record of temperatures in your own garden.

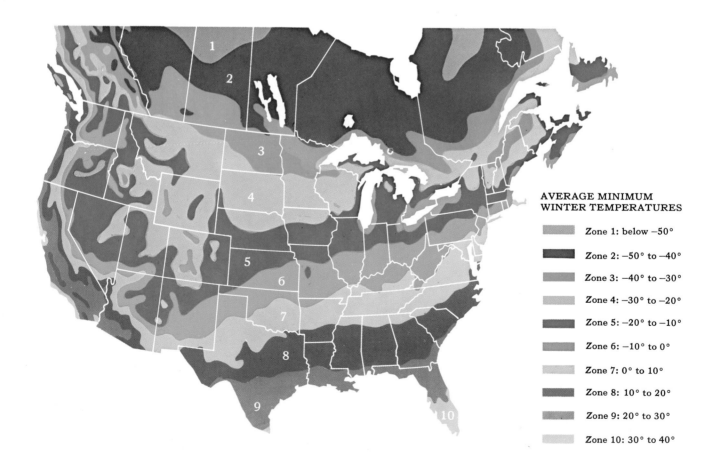

AVERAGE MINIMUM WINTER TEMPERATURES

Zone 1: below −50°

Zone 2: −50° to −40°

Zone 3: −40° to −30°

Zone 4: −30° to −20°

Zone 5: −20° to −10°

Zone 6: −10° to 0°

Zone 7: 0° to 10°

Zone 8: 10° to 20°

Zone 9: 20° to 30°

Zone 10: 30° to 40°

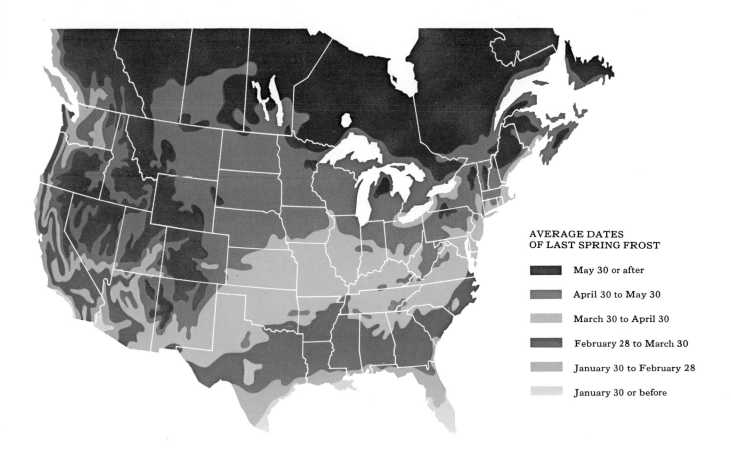

AVERAGE DATES
OF LAST SPRING FROST

■ May 30 or after

■ April 30 to May 30

■ March 30 to April 30

■ February 28 to March 30

■ January 30 to February 28

■ January 30 or before

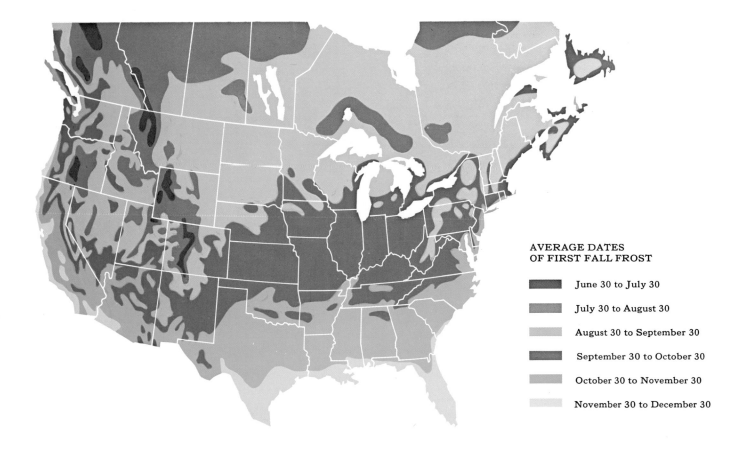

AVERAGE DATES
OF FIRST FALL FROST

■ June 30 to July 30

■ July 30 to August 30

■ August 30 to September 30

■ September 30 to October 30

■ October 30 to November 30

■ November 30 to December 30

Characteristics of 126 herbs

	USES									PROPAGATION				PLANT TYPE			SOIL NEEDS		LIGHT NEEDS		HEIGHT			
	Culinary seasonings	Salad greens	Teas	Fragrances	Dried arrangements	Decorative foliage	Decorative flowers	Source of bee nectar	House plants	Seeds	Stem cuttings	Bulbs	Root divisions	Hardy perennial	Tender perennial	Annual or biennial	Dry	Wet to moist	Direct sunlight	Shade or partial shade	Under 1 foot	1 to 3 feet	3 to 5 feet	Over 5 feet
ACHILLEA MILLEFOLIUM (yarrow)			●	●			●			●			●	●			●		●			●		
ACORUS CALAMUS (sweet flag)	●		●							●			●	●				●	●			●		
AGASTACHE FOENICULUM (anise hyssop)	●		●	●				●		●			●	●				●	●			●		
AGRIMONIA EUPATORIA (agrimony)			●	●						●			●	●			●		●	●		●		
AJUGA REPTANS (ajuga)						●				●			●	●			●	●	●	●	●			
ALCHEMILLA VULGARIS (lady's mantle)				●	●			●	●	●			●					●		●	●			
ALLIUM ASCALONICUM (shallot)	●	●					●		●			●	●				●		●			●		
ALLIUM CEPA AGGREGATUM (top onion)	●	●			●			●				●	●				●		●			●		
ALLIUM PORRUM (leek)	●	●						●								●	●	●	●					
ALLIUM SATIVUM (garlic)	●	●						●				●	●	●				●	●			●		
ALLIUM SCHOENOPRASUM (chive)	●	●					●			●		●	●	●				●	●		●			
ALOE VERA (aloe)						●			●		●		●		●		●		●			●	●	
ALTHAEA OFFICINALIS (marsh mallow)		●					●			●			●		●		●	●	●				●	
ANCHUSA OFFICINALIS (alkanet)	●					●	●			●				●		●	●		●			●		
ANEMONE PULSATILLA (pasque flower)							●			●			●				●	●	●	●	●			
ANETHUM GRAVEOLENS (dill)	●	●				●	●			●						●	●		●			●		
ANGELICA ARCHANGELICA (angelica)	●		●							●			●	●		●		●		●			●	●
ANTHEMIS NOBILIS (chamomile)	●		●	●				●		●			●	●				●	●		●			
ANTHRISCUS CEREFOLIUM (chervil)	●	●				●				●						●		●	●	●	●			
ARMORACIA RUSTICANA (horseradish)	●												●	●			●	●	●			●		
ARTEMISIA ABSINTHIUM (wormwood)			●	●	●			●	●				●	●			●		●			●	●	
ARTEMISIA DRACUNCULUS (tarragon)	●								●		●		●		●		●		●			●		
ASPERULA ODORATA (woodruff)	●			●		●	●		●	●			●	●				●		●	●			
ATRIPLEX HORTENSIS (orach)		●				●				●						●	●	●	●					●
BAPTISIA TINCTORIA (wild indigo)						●	●			●					●		●		●			●		
BARBAREA VULGARIS (winter cress)	●	●								●			●			●	●		●			●		
BORAGO OFFICINALIS (borage)	●	●	●					●		●						●	●		●			●		
BRASSICA ALBA (white mustard)	●	●						●		●						●	●		●			●		
CALENDULA OFFICINALIS (calendula)						●		●	●	●						●	●		●			●		
CARTHAMUS TINCTORIUS (safflower)	●				●					●						●	●		●			●		
CARUM CARVI (caraway)	●		●							●						●	●		●			●		
CASSIA MARILANDICA (wild senna)						●	●			●					●		●		●	●			●	●
CHENOPODIUM BONUS-HENRICUS (Good-King-Henry)	●	●						●	●			●	●			●	●		●			●		
CHENOPODIUM BOTRYS (ambrosia)			●	●	●					●					●		●		●			●		
CHRYSANTHEMUM BALSAMITA TANACETOIDES (costmary)	●	●		●				●	●				●	●		●	●	●	●			●		
CICHORIUM INTYBUS (chicory)	●	●				●	●	●	●					●			●	●	●				●	●
CITRUS MITIS (calamondin orange)				●				●	●	●					●			●	●			●		
CNICUS BENEDICTUS (blessed thistle)						●	●			●					●	●	●		●			●		
CORIANDRUM SATIVUM (coriander)	●			●						●						●	●		●			●		
CRITHMUM MARITIMUM (samphire)	●	●	●			●			●	●	●		●		●		●		●		●			
CROCUS SATIVUS (saffron crocus)	●						●					●			●		●		●			●		
CUMINUM CYMINUM (cumin)	●					●				●						●	●		●			●		
CYNARA CARDUNCULUS (cardoon)							●			●					●	●		●	●	●			●	
DICTAMNUS ALBUS (gas plant)				●			●			●				●			●		●			●		
DIGITALIS PURPUREA (foxglove)							●	●		●						●	●		●				●	
DIPSACUS SYLVESTRIS (teasel)					●		●			●						●	●	●	●					●
FILIPENDULA HEXAPETALA (dropwort)				●		●	●	●		●			●	●			●	●	●			●		
FOENICULUM VULGARE (fennel)	●	●	●	●				●		●			●	●			●		●				●	●
FOENICULUM VULGARE DULCE (finochio)		●								●			●		●	●	●		●			●		
FUMARIA OFFICINALIS (fumitory)						●	●			●					●	●			●		●			

152

Table — Herb reference chart (Galium verum through Salvia officinalis)

Plant	Culinary seasonings	Salad greens	Teas	Fragrances	Dried arrangements	Decorative foliage	Decorative flowers	Source of bee nectar	House plants	Seeds	Stem cuttings	Bulbs	Root divisions	Hardy perennial	Tender perennial	Annual or biennial	Dry	Wet to moist	Direct sunlight	Shade or partial shade	Under 1 foot	1 to 3 feet	3 to 5 feet	Over 5 feet
GALIUM VERUM (yellow bedstraw)				●	●		●	●		●	●			●		●	●	●	●		●			
GERANIUM ROBERTIANUM (herb Robert)					●			●								●		●	●	●	●			
HELIOTROPIUM PERUVIANUM (common heliotrope)				●			●	●	●	●				●	●			●	●		●			
HYSSOPUS OFFICINALIS (hyssop)			●			●	●	●		●	●					●			●		●			
INULA HELENIUM (elecampane)	●		●			●		●		●	●					●	●	●	●				●	●
IRIS GERMANICA FLORENTINA (orris)			●			●		●		●	●				●				●		●	●		
ISATIS TINCTORIA (woad)			●			●		●		●				●	●			●	●			●	●	
JASMINUM OFFICINALE (jasmine)			●			●		●			●				●		●		●				●	●
LAMIUM MACULATUM (spotted dead nettle)				●	●	●	●		●		●	●						●	●	●				
LAURUS NOBILIS (sweet bay)	●		●	●	●			●		●				●			●	●	●	●			●	●
LAVANDULA DENTATA (fringed lavender)			●		●	●	●	●	●		●			●			●		●			●		
LAVANDULA OFFICINALIS (English lavender)			●	●	●	●	●	●	●	●	●			●			●		●			●		
LAVANDULA STOECHAS (French lavender)			●	●	●		●	●	●		●			●			●		●			●		
LEPIDIUM SATIVUM (garden cress)	●	●						●							●	●		●	●			●		
LEVISTICUM OFFICINALE (lovage)	●	●						●		●	●						●	●	●				●	●
LIPPIA CITRIODORA (lemon verbena)	●		●	●	●			●		●					●		●		●				●	●
MARRUBIUM VULGARE (horehound)			●		●	●		●		●				●			●		●			●		
MATRICARIA CHAMOMILLA (German chamomile)			●	●				●		●					●	●	●		●			●		
MELISSA OFFICINALIS (balm)	●		●	●		●		●	●	●	●			●			●	●	●			●		
MENTHA PIPERITA OFFICINALIS (peppermint)	●		●	●					●	●	●							●	●	●		●		
MENTHA PULEGIUM (pennyroyal)			●	●					●	●			●	●				●	●	●	●			
MENTHA ROTUNDIFOLIA (apple mint)	●		●	●		●	●		●		●							●	●			●		
MENTHA SPICATA (spearmint)	●	●	●	●					●		●							●	●			●		
MONARDA DIDYMA (bee balm)	●		●	●			●	●		●	●							●	●			●		
MYRRHIS ODORATA (sweet cicely)	●	●		●			●	●		●	●							●	●			●		
MYRTUS COMMUNIS (myrtle)	●			●			●		●		●				●		●	●	●	●		●	●	●
NASTURTIUM OFFICINALE (watercress)		●						●	●				●					●	●	●		●		
NEPETA CATARIA (catnip)			●	●			●	●	●				●	●			●		●			●		
NIGELLA SATIVA (fennel flower)	●					●			●						●	●	●		●			●		
OCIMUM BASILICUM (sweet basil)	●	●	●	●			●	●	●	●						●		●	●			●		
OCIMUM BASILICUM 'DARK OPAL' (purple basil)	●	●		●	●			●	●	●						●		●	●			●		
ORIGANUM DICTAMNUS (dittany of Crete)	●	●	●	●		●	●	●		●					●		●		●		●			
ORIGANUM MAJORANA (sweet marjoram)	●			●		●	●	●	●	●					●	●	●		●		●			
ORIGANUM VULGARE (wild marjoram)	●		●	●		●	●	●		●	●			●	●		●	●	●			●		
OSMANTHUS FRAGRANS (sweet olive)			●					●	●		●				●			●		●		●	●	●
PELARGONIUM 'CLORINDA' (clorinda geranium)	●		●			●		●	●		●				●		●		●			●		
PELARGONIUM CRISPUM (lemon-scented geranium)	●		●					●	●		●				●		●		●			●		
PELARGONIUM GRAVEOLENS (rose-scented geranium)	●		●		●			●	●		●				●		●		●				●	
PELARGONIUM TOMENTOSUM (peppermint-scented geranium)	●		●		●			●	●	●	●				●		●		●				●	
PERILLA FRUTESCENS CRISPA (purple perilla)	●	●		●	●				●							●		●	●			●		
PETROSELINUM CRISPUM (parsley)	●	●						●	●	●						●		●	●	●	●			
PETROSELINUM FELICINUM (Italian parsley)	●	●						●	●	●						●		●	●			●		
PIMPINELLA ANISUM (anise)	●		●					●		●						●	●		●			●		
PRIMULA VERIS (cowslip)		●	●					●		●		●	●					●		●	●	●		
ROSA DAMASCENA (damask rose)	●		●	●			●				●			●				●	●				●	
ROSA GALLICA (French rose)	●		●	●			●				●			●				●	●			●	●	
ROSMARINUS OFFICINALIS (rosemary)	●		●	●		●	●	●	●	●	●				●		●		●	●		●	●	●
RUMEX SCUTATUS (French sorrel)	●	●			●			●					●					●	●			●		
RUTA GRAVEOLENS (rue)				●	●	●		●		●				●	●		●		●			●		
SALVIA OFFICINALIS (sage)	●		●	●			●	●	●	●	●							●	●	●		●		

	Culinary seasonings	Salad greens	Teas	Fragrances	Dried arrangements	Decorative foliage	Decorative flowers	Source of bee nectar	House plants	Seeds	Stem cuttings	Bulbs	Root divisions	Hardy perennial	Tender perennial	Annual or biennial	Dry	Wet to moist	Direct sunlight	Shade or partial shade	Under 1 foot	1 to 3 feet	3 to 5 feet	Over 5 feet
	USES									PROPAGATION				PLANT TYPE			SOIL NEEDS		LIGHT NEEDS		HEIGHT			
SALVIA RUTILANS (pineapple sage)				•			•	•	•		•		•		•		•	•	•	•		•		
SANGUISORBA MINOR (burnet)	•	•	•					•	•		•		•	•			•		•			•		
SANTOLINA CHAMAECYPARISSUS (lavender cotton)				•	•	•	•		•		•		•	•	•	•		•	•			•		
SATUREIA HORTENSIS (summer savory)	•		•	•			•	•	•	•			•			•	•	•	•			•		
SATUREIA MONTANA (winter savory)	•		•	•			•	•	•	•			•	•			•		•		•			
SEMPERVIVUM TECTORUM (houseleek)							•		•		•	•	•		•		•		•		•			
SESAMUM INDICUM (sesame)	•							•						•	•	•	•		•					
SILYBUM MARIANUM (St. Mary's thistle)				•					•					•	•	•	•		•					
SIUM SISARUM (skirret)	•							•			•	•		•			•		•		•	•		
STACHYS OFFICINALIS (wood betony)		•	•			•		•			•	•		•			•		•		•			
STACHYS OLYMPICA (lamb's ears)				•				•			•	•		•			•		•		•			
SYMPHYTUM OFFICINALE (comfrey)	•	•	•			•	•		•		•	•				•	•	•			•			
TANACETUM VULGARE (tansy)			•	•	•		•		•		•	•				•	•	•			•	•		
TARAXACUM OFFICINALE (dandelion)	•	•	•					•			•	•			•	•		•			•			
TEUCRIUM CHAMAEDRYS (germander)						•		•	•		•	•			•		•		•		•			
THYMUS CITRIODORUS (lemon thyme)	•		•	•			•		•		•	•			•		•		•		•			
THYMUS SERPYLLUM (wild thyme)		•	•		•		•	•	•		•	•			•		•		•		•			
THYMUS VULGARIS (common thyme)	•		•	•			•	•	•	•		•	•			•	•			•				
TRIGONELLA FOENUM-GRAECUM (fenugreek)	•		•				•				•	•		•		•		•						
TROPAEOLUM MAJUS (nasturtium)	•	•			•	•		•	•			•		•	•		•		•					•
TUSSILAGO FARFARA (coltsfoot)			•					•			•	•				•	•	•			•			
VALERIANA OFFICINALIS (valerian)			•	•	•	•		•			•	•				•	•		•				•	
VERBASCUM THAPSUS (great mullein)			•		•			•			•	•		•	•		•		•				•	•
VERONICA OFFICINALIS (common speedwell)			•					•			•	•		•		•		•	•	•				
VIOLA ODORATA (sweet violet)	•	•		•		•		•	•		•	•		•		•		•		•	•			
VIOLA TRICOLOR (Johnny-jump-up)	•	•		•			•		•	•		•			•	•		•		•	•			

Picture credits

The sources for the illustrations in this book are shown below. Credits from left to right are separated by semicolons, from top to bottom by dashes. Cover—Marina Schinz, courtesy Brooklyn Botanic Garden. 4—Courtesy of WGBH Educational Foundation; Sarah Tanner; Richard Crist. 6—Derek Bayes, by permission of the Provost and Fellows of Eton College. 10, 11—Drawings by Matt Greene. 14, 15—Enrico Ferorelli. 18, 19—David Lees. 24—Fred De Van. 26 through 37—Drawings by Matt Greene. 41, 42, 43—Marina Schinz. 44—Fleming B. Fuller—Bob Waterman. 45—Fleming B. Fuller—John Perella. 46, 47—Enrico Ferorelli. 48, 49—Marina Schinz. 50—Enrico Ferorelli—Marina Schinz. 51—Marina Schinz—Enrico Ferorelli. 52, 53—Marina Schinz; Patrick Thurston. 54—Sonja Bullaty and Angelo Lomeo. 56, 58—Drawings by Matt Greene. 60 through 63—Ken Kay. 65, 66—Drawings by Matt Greene. 68—Peter B. Kaplan. 71 through 79—Drawings by Matt Greene. 81—Sonja Bullaty and Angelo Lomeo. 82—Marina Schinz; Sonja Bullaty and Angelo Lomeo—Al Satterwhite. 83—Sonja Bullaty and Angelo Lomeo. 84—Al Satterwhite; Sonja Bullaty and Angelo Lomeo. 85—Marina Schinz except bottom right Peter B. Kaplan. 90 through 149—Encyclopedia illustrations by Richard Crist. 150, 151—Maps by Adolph E. Brotman.

Acknowledgments

The index for this book was prepared by Sara Hannum Chase. For their help in the preparation of this book, the editors wish to thank the following: Jean Blackburn, American Association of Nurserymen, Washington, D.C.; Gavin Bridson, Linnean Society, London; Dr. Henry Cathey, U.S. Department of Agriculture, Washington, D.C.; Sergio Chiesa, Institute of Botany and Plant Physiology, University of Padua, Italy; Marie Therese Colonna, Falls Church, Va.; Mrs. David L. Conger, Stonington, Conn.; Bernard Currid, Brooklyn Botanic Garden, Brooklyn, N.Y.; Patrick Devlin, Keeper of College Library

154

and Collections, Eton College, England; Gertrude B. Foster, Falls Village, Conn.; Jane Opper Grace, New York City; Barbara Heinon, Horticultural Society of New York, New York City; The Herb Society of America, Boston, Mass.; Richard Holiman, Coventry, Conn.; Mrs. Frederic P. Houston, New York City; Mrs. Walter K. Howard, Wayne, Pa.; Dr. Peter Hyytio, L. H. Bailey Hortorium, Cornell University, Ithaca, N.Y.; Dr. N. R. Ker, F.B.A., Edinburgh; Giangiacomo Lorenzoni, Institute of Botany and Plant Physiology, University of Padua, Italy; The Marchioness of Salisbury, Cranborne Manor, Dorset, England; Judge Peter Mason, London; Polly Murray, McCormick and Co., Inc., Baltimore, Md.; Giampaolo Porlezza, Como, Italy; Robin Price, Wellcome Institute for the History of Medicine, London; Mrs. J. Pancost Reath, Radnor, Pa.; Mrs. George A. Reed, Jr., Malvern, Pa.; Paolo Rovesti, President, Centro Italiano Per L'Erboristeria, Milan; John Sales, National Trust, London; Kay Sanecki, Tring, Hertfordshire, England; Elizabeth Scholtz, Director, Brooklyn Botanic Garden, Brooklyn, N.Y.; Diane Schwartz, The New York Botanical Garden, Bronx, N.Y.; Dr. Malcolm Stewart, Society of Herbalists, London; Milton Taylor, Manager, Caswell-Massey, Ltd., New York City; Mrs. Charles S. Truitt, Haverford, Pa.; Rosemary Verey, Barnsley House, Gloucestershire, England; W. Williams, Department of Prints and Drawings, British Museum, London; Betty Wylder, Long Beach, Calif.

Bibliography

Bailey, L. H., *The Standard Cyclopedia of Horticulture* (3 vols.). Macmillan Publishing Company, Inc., 1900.

Brooklyn Botanic Garden, *Handbook on Herbs*. BBG, 1971.

Brooklyn Botanic Garden, *Herbs and Their Ornamental Uses*. BBG, 1972.

Campbell, Mary Mason, *Betty Crocker's Kitchen Gardens*. Western Publishing Co., Inc., 1971.

Chittenden, Fred J., *The Royal Horticultural Society Dictionary of Gardening*. Clarendon Press, 1974.

Clarkson, Rosetta E., *Herbs: Their Culture and Uses*. Macmillan Publishing Company, Inc., 1942.

Clarkson, Rosetta E., *The Golden Age of Herbs and Herbalists*. Dover Pubns., Inc., 1972. (Reprint of *Green Enchantment*. Macmillan Company, Inc., 1940.)

Culpeper, Nicholas, *The English Physitian Enlarged*. Peter Cole, 1656.

Dioscorides, Pedanius, *Greek Herbal*. Ed. by Robert T. Gunther, translated by John Goodyear. Hafner Press, 1968. (Reprint of 1933 ed.)

Doole, Louise Evans, *Herbs for Health: How to Grow and Use Them*. Wilshire, 1962.

Elbert, Virginia F. and George A., *Fun with Growing Herbs Indoors*. Crown Pubs., Inc., 1974.

Foster, Gertrude B., *Herbs for Every Garden*. E. P. Dutton & Co., Inc., 1966.

Fox, Helen Morgenthau, *Gardening with Herbs for Flavor and Fragrance*. Macmillan Publishing Company, Inc., 1953.

Graf, Alfred Byrd, *Exotica*. Roehrs Company Inc., 1957.

Grieve, Mrs. M., *A Modern Herbal* (2 vols.). Hafner Press, 1971.

Hall, Dorothy, *The Book of Herbs*. Charles Scribner's Sons, 1972.

Herb Society of America, *Herbs for Use and for Delight*. Dover Pubns., Inc., 1974.

Herb Society of America, *A Primer for Herb Growing*. HSA, 1966.

Herb Society of America, *Simple Rules for Herb Cookery*. HSA, 1954.

Hériteau, Jacqueline, *Herbs*. Grosset & Dunlap, Inc., 1975.

Hoffman, Irene Botsford, *The Book of Herb Cookery*. Gramercy Publishing Company, 1940.

Hylton, William H., and others, *The Rodale Herb Book*. Rodale Press Books, Inc., 1974.

Loewenfeld, Claire, and Back, Philippa, *The Complete Book of Herbs and Spices*. G. P. Putnam's Sons, 1974.

Loewenfeld, Claire, and Back, Philippa, *Herbs, Health and Cookery*. Universal Publishing & Distributing Corp., 1970.

Mazza, Irma Goodrich, *Herbs for the Kitchen*. Little, Brown & Co., 1975.

Miloradovich, Milo, *Art of Cooking with Herbs and Spices*. Doubleday & Co., Inc., 1950.

Muenscher, Walter Conrad, and Rice, Myron Arthur, *Garden Spice and Wild Pot-Herbs*. Comstock Editions, Inc., 1955.

Northcote, Lady Rosalind, *The Book of Herb Lore*. Dover Pubns., Inc., 1971.

Sanecki, Kay N., *The Complete Book of Herbs*. Macmillan Publishing Company, Inc., 1974.

Schafer, Violet, *Herbcraft*. Yerba Buena Press, 1971.

Simmons, Adelma G., *Herb Gardening in Five Seasons*. Hawthorn Books, Inc., 1964.

Simmons, Adelma G., *Herb Gardens of Delight*. Hawthorn Books, Inc., 1974.

Simmons, Adelma G., *Herbs to Grow Indoors*. Hawthorn Books, Inc., 1969.

Simmons, Adelma G., *A Merry Christmas Herbal*. William Morrow & Co., Inc., 1968.

Sunset Books, *Cooking with Spices and Herbs*. Lane Publishing Co., 1974.

Sunset Books, *How to Grow Herbs*. Lane Publishing Co., 1972.

Taylor, Norman, ed., *Encyclopedia of Gardening*. Houghton Mifflin Company, 1936.

Webster, Helen, *Herbs: How to Grow Them and How to Use Them*. Charles T. Branford Co., 1942.

Wyman, Donald, *Wyman's Gardening Encyclopedia*. Macmillan Publishing Company, Inc., 1971.

Index

Numerals in italics indicate an illustration of the subject mentioned

PRINTED IN U.S.A.